The Culinary Camper

Barbara Tidwell

The Culinary Camper
By Barbara Tidwell
Copyright © 2014

ISBN-13: 978-1494943424
ISBN-10: 1494943425

Printed in the United States of America

Contents

Preface

As I write these first few sentences of this book, I'm gazing out across the water from my campsite in the beautiful Deception Pass area of Washington State. It's a gorgeous late spring weekend with friends. I crawled out of my pop up camper this morning to find bright blue skies, the morning mist already burning off, the smell of coffee, and whiffs of pine needles drifting in the air. For breakfast, I prepared delicious egg, cheese, and sausage pocket sandwiches over the fire. We were just licking the last crumbs off of our fingers when a friend suddenly looked up and said, "This is so good! You should write a cookbook!"

She continued, specifying that it should not be just any cookbook – it should be a cookbook focused on camp cooking. My interest was piqued because not only do I love to cook, but I really love to cook at a campfire. It's a different type of challenge trying to cook outdoors and master it.

My favorite recipe to share with you is the River Chicken. You are probably wondering what a "River Chicken" is. It all started back in 1987 when I went on a camping trip with two friends up to Box Canyon, Washington. This was my first camping trip with these particular friends. One friend insisted upon making a whole chicken on a spit, saying it would be the best chicken we had ever eaten. As we had brought only the most basic of camping foods, including the campsite staple of hot dogs, we readily agreed he should make this. We watched in fascination as he gathered up two large Y-shaped branches and stuck them into the ground on either side of the campfire. He then found a third stick, stripped it of bark, and placed it in the river to soak while he cleaned the chicken. Once the chicken was ready he bound it with some twine, skewered it on the well soaked third stick, and then he suspended the whole thing between the two forked branches just over the crackling fire.

Even though we were awed by what he had created, my friend suddenly realized that he had unfortunately forgotten to bring any spices. We didn't even have salt or pepper. Someone got the brilliant idea to crush the chips we were eating and use them on the chicken. Since we had no other spice options we went for it, and rubbed the crushed salted chips on the chicken as it cooked. It worked amazingly well, and the chicken turned out to be just as described - the best we had ever eaten. From that point on, I was hooked on the recipe and was destined to reproduce it again and again on future camping trips.

It was a couple of years later that a larger group of us including two young children, 5 and 2 years of age, went camping. I planned to make the spit-roasted chicken for dinner. While everybody was resting, I took the chicken down to the river to clean as usual. After it was prepped, I skewered it and headed back. As I was walking back into camp, the two children saw me walking up the hill and were amazed that I had come up from the river with a bird on a stick. The older child asked me with wide eyes where I had gotten it. At this point I couldn't resist the chance to pull her leg a little bit. I told the children that my old Native American friend had taught me how to catch "River Chicken" and that is what I had been doing. She believed every word.

Needless to say, all the adults found this hilarious, and "River Chicken" became an inside joke for years to come. One friend wrote a song parody called "Lament of the River Chicken," and another friend turned old fishing licenses into mock River Chicken hunting licenses. To this day, the mention of River Chicken within my circle of friends brings smiles and fond memories.

Within *The Culinary Camper*, you will find the River Chicken recipe along with many other wonderful recipes and fond camping memories. In this book, I will share with you recipes and a few stories from camping trips during my youth, as a camp counselor, an assistant camp cook, and being the camp chef for countless weekends I have spent in the woods with friends. Through the years, I have gathered a rich pool of experiences from which to draw in creating this book.

Cooks for larger organized camps will find some interesting recipes that can be altered for larger crowds. Camp counselors going with their campers out for overnights will find many tasty and fun ideas for desert. Of course, the generalist camper who loves to eat well while camping will find many delicious recipes to try. *The Culinary Camper* is for anyone who wants to experiment and try new things while camping.

The times that I have spent camping with friends and family have been some of the best times of my life. Friends I camped with in high school, college, and as a camp counselor are still my friends decades later. The fond memories I created with them are the inspiration for this book. I hope that they will find lots of memories to make them smile and salivate once again in these pages. I hope that you, my fellow camp cooks, can use *The Culinary Camper* to create wonderful memories of your own. Sit around a campfire, bask in the warmth of friends and family, enjoy great food, and make memories that last a lifetime.

Stovetop and Campfire Cooking

While a lot of this book is very centered on campfire cooking, using a camp stove is also fun and can be extremely handy when cooking certain items. Truth be told, it is easier to control prolonged heat over a camp stove than a campfire. The key is have a good camp stove that does not produce so many BTU's that it burns everything to a crisp or a stove that does not have enough power to boil water. To address this, I've added a section to the appendix on choosing a good camp stove. When I am camp cook, I like to use both campfire and stove.

I also sit in my Class A RV as I write much of this book which has its own gas stove and oven. While I prefer to cook outside, I'm glad to have these items in the winter since I live full time in my RV. Cooking in an RV has its own challenges. Mostly dealing with moisture caused by cooking and secondly with the odd way the oven is configured for cooking with the heating element in the middle of the oven.

It should go without saying, but I think it is of most importance to remember that you are in essence playing with fire when cooking over an open flame. Please use all cautions necessary including fire proof gloves, and eyewear. Always keep a burn kit, first aid kit, and a fire extinguisher or bucket of water nearby. Please accept the risk you take in working with open flames, be careful, and have a lot of fun. Neither I nor the publisher of this book assumes any responsibility for any accidents or losses endured while following these recipes.

This is how I cook

These recipes are a starting point for any cooking endeavor. I often change a recipe to try something new. If you should ever meet me in a campground cooking away, you may see me doing everything somewhat differently than I have in print. I love to experiment with my cooking and I encourage you to do the same. I see recipes as a guide upon which there is always room for improvement.

Preparing ahead of time at home

Some recipes are just easier to prep at home and bring camping to cook over the fire. Cooking over the fire is fun and gives food a wonderful smoky flavor, but not everything has to be done at the campsite. I've tried to specify that with each recipe to prep at home when it makes things easier. Being a camping foodie, I painstakingly re-evaluated my recipe selection to make sure these were not too difficult for the average camper knowing that most people like to keep the camping menu simple. There are still a few difficult recipes in this book for those who want the challenge.

Contact Me

If you like this book, you may find more recipes on my web site at culinarycamper.com. You also may contact me on Twitter @culinarycamper or on Facebook.

Feel free to login to the website at culinarycamper.com and add your own favorite recipe. Be it for an outdoor feast or a simple hot dog on a stick, your input is valued. You can also contact me through the Contact page and leave any feedback for improving the site or this book.

Volume Purchasing

If you would like to buy more than ten copies of this book at a time, contact me on my website culinarycamper.com by clicking the Contact menu and submitting the contact form. Please let me know how many copies you are interested in.

Acknowledgements

Lastly I want to say thanks to all those who were instrumental in helping get this book done. Thank you to Jodene, my best friend, for giving me the idea to write it, being my sounding board, and giving me feedback for so many of the recipes I included. Thanks to Jolene, Kerry, and Tamryn for their contributions to the creation of this book. A special thanks to my friends and family who have enjoyed my cooking enough to encourage me to finish this project.

1
Gear

There is something about being out-of-doors that is not only exhilarating, but also captivating and relaxing. I try to spend as much time as possible outside because I tend to get a little stir-crazy when I'm cooped up inside for too long. When I am out camping, I am a bit of a "gear geek." I love my toys, from my new ultra-lightweight fishing rod to my well-used 12 inch cast iron skillet. I have found that the right equipment can be a huge advantage in campfire cooking, so I'm going to begin by talking about what gear you might want to bring with you for a camp cookout. Of course, you would need a whole chuck wagon for all the stuff I am going to mention here, so I would suggest choosing only what you need to bring based on what you plan to cook.

Enjoyable camping, especially camp cooking, requires some planning. You should choose your meals while keeping in mind the amount of gear you'll need to bring to prepare them. The amount of gear you need for many of these recipes will make them only suitable for car camping, so careful planning is very necessary if you are working with less space. In general, the more overlap there is between the gear that you need for each meal the better, but if there are special things you would like to create, by all means plan to bring the specialty equipment along. Of course, you don't want to have so much overlap that you're trying to cook four different things all at once in the same pot. Keep in mind that the gear you bring must be packed, unpacked for use, cleaned, and packed again for the trip home.

In *The Culinary Camper*, I have listed the equipment that you will need in order to make the recipe. This should help guide you in what you should pack for your trip. I am of the opinion that anything you can cook at home or on a grill you can cook at a camp site, but I say this with the caveat that some meals are more complicated than others. With the right tools, it can be a fun and rewarding experience. Your friends will think you are the coolest thing alive for producing all sorts of delicious food while in the wilderness. Food always tastes better around a campfire.

Essential Gear

Here are the basic pieces of gear one should always have for camp cooking:

- **First Aid Kit:** You should **never** go out into the woods without a well-stocked first aid kit.

- **Potable Water:** Always bring more than you think you will need, unless you are **sure** there is a safe water source near your campsite or you have a method to sterilize it.

- **Pot Holders, Oven Mitts, or Leather Gloves:** They should be thick work gloves, not walk around the town looking nice gloves.

- **Waterproof Matches or Lighter:** Long ignition sources that can extend into small places, such as fireplaces matches or long-barrel butane lighters, are often useful.

- **Spatula:** Ideally you should have both a flexible and a non-flexible metal spatula.

- **Skillet:** I recommend at least a 12 inch skillet and cast iron is my favorite.

- **Cooking Pot:** Your pot should be able to hold at least 2 quarts liquid, but 4 or more is better. Not only is this useful for cooking in but it is also useful for heating water for dishes.

- **Good Knife and Cutting Board:** Be sure it is reasonably sharp or bring a small sharpener. Dull knives cause mishaps.

- **Tongs:** These are great for grabbing items out of a fire.

- **Spices:** Because of the limitations of campground cooking, herbs in *The Culinary Camper* recipes should always be considered to be dried, unless otherwise specified. Always have salt and pepper on hand.

- **Sealable Plastic Food Storage:** Bags or hard-sided containers or both

- **Sturdy Cooler:** In many wilderness areas, there are animals such as raccoons and bears that will go after any 'people food' to which they have even a hint of access. Bears have even been known to attempt to break into cars if they have been acclimated to the availability of food. The safest way to store your food is in an air-tight cooler inside your vehicle. If that isn't an option because of your location, then either suspend your food on ropes high above the ground between two trees, at a slight distance from your campsite. You can also use bear proof containers that either the campground provides or you can buy a smaller version. Be sure you get all food secured before leaving your campsite or going to bed!

- **Tarp:** A good tarp or three will keep firewood dry, shelter you and your supplies from rain, and prevent paper towels, plates, and other items from turning into sodden, useless lumps.

- **Towels:** Be aware that food smells remaining on cloth towels after cleanup may draw unwelcome visitors during the night. Paper towels, while less environmentally friendly, are easily disposed of in the campfire after meals.

- **Dish Soap:** Dishes should be cleaned after meals to avoid drawing animal attention. Use a biodegradable soap, and do not use harsh detergents or the same dish soap you may use in the home.

- **Trash Bags:** Please, **never** leave messes behind! It sets a bad example, creates an ugly, smelly scene for the next camper, and is bad for the environment. It also teaches wild animals to seek out human campsites which can lead to dangerous encounters.

- **Aluminum Foil:** There are lots of camp recipes to be made using foil. Using aluminum foil saves on dishes and is a great way to make packing lighter and easier.

- **Food Thermometer:** I like to use one when making chicken or other meats so that I know the meat is safe to eat.

- **Bleach Wipes or handy wipes:** You may need to sanitize an area or your hands. These work great for sanitizing.

- **Firewood:** While it is often possible to collect dry wood around a campsite, having wood that is guaranteed to be dry can avoid a lot of frustration and wasted time. Bring at least a few bundles per night you plan to stay.

- **Hatchet or Hand Saw:** When seeking wood, find trees that have already fallen and are seasoned. Wood from freshly cut trees will be wet and thus will not burn well. In addition, cutting living trees simply isn't an eco-friendly practice and may be illegal in many places.

Optional Gear

These are things I often bring along on camp cookouts. Some of them are essential to specific kinds of recipes; others simply add convenience.

- **Plastic Totes:** These are great for staying organized and tidy at the campsite. When left sealed for the night, they can protect food or other items from small critters.

- **Cooking Spoon:** Ideally you should have both a slotted and a regular spoon. This becomes a necessity if you are making anything in a pot.

- **Twine:** Both food grade and general purpose for tying up tarps or hanging food.

- **Measuring Cups and Spoons:** The recipes in *The Culinary Camper* use measuring cups and spoons should be assumed to be necessary equipment without being listed.

- **Folding Table:** Upon arrival at the campsite, you may find that the picnic table is not necessarily big enough for all you need. Bring at least one small folding table for assisting in cooking tasks.

- **Apron:** An apron will protect your clothes from dirt, grease, and flying sparks, and prevents loose garments from falling into the coals or flames as you cook.

- **Water Purifier:** At least have a method planned for water purification. If all else fails, have a backup plan with a water purifier or be able to boil your water in a pot to purify it.

- **Gas Camping Stove:** Be sure you check for an empty gas tank before you leave civilization!

- **Dutch Oven:** A heavy cook pot, usually cast iron, with a tight fitting lid. There are two kinds of Dutch ovens. The Flat-bottomed Dutch oven is made for use on a cook top or in an oven. The cowboy, or chuck wagon variety, typically has a wire bail handle, 3 small legs to allow it to be set over coals, and a slightly concave top which allows coals to be placed on the lid.

- **Pie Iron:** A pie iron, often called a sandwich maker, is a cooking tool consisting of two hinged metal plates, either aluminum or cast iron, which form a compartment when closed. Each plate is attached to a long handle so that food placed inside may be held over the fire, heated, and then flipped over to cook the other side. Pie irons are used for heating items, such as toast, sandwiches, and pies which have layers of bread or pastry.

- **Skewers:** The longer the better, skewers are useful for cooking hotdogs, marshmallows, shish kebobs, etc. Wooden ones should be soaked before use.

- **Rotisserie:** A rotisserie can be constructed out of a few simple sticks, but a mechanical spit with a crank will greatly ease the process of getting an evenly cooked dish. I love my battery operated rotisserie.

- **Rotisserie Forks:** A spit fork is a small piece of metal with four bent prongs, making it look somewhat like a spider, and is used to secure items on a spit. I highly recommend getting them.

- **Portable Grill:** You may not be able to build a fire all the time so a grill works great for cooking when no fire is allowed.

- **Beer Butt Chicken Roaster:** A stand that holds a chicken upright on top of an open beer can is one of my favorite ways to roast a chicken.

- **Large Mixing Bowl:** This is handy for many things such as doing dishes, mixing cakes or any other use you may find.

- **Colander** You will want this if you plan to make pasta.

- **Wire Whisk:** Whisks are great for mixing items such as eggs or for making gravy.

- **Scrub Brush:** To clean pots and pans you may need a soft scrub brush to get out cooked in food.

Cast Iron Care

Cast iron cookware is a wonderful accoutrement for the outdoor, or indeed, indoor, chef. Naturally non-stick when used and maintained properly, cast iron can add trace amounts of iron to food. Its best quality is that it heats evenly and thoroughly. It does, however, require a type of treatment unique among cookware. Cast iron pans are almost never meant to be washed (aside from possibly at first usage). Instead, they must be seasoned, which means melting lard into tiny crevices in the metal. Done properly, this will keep your cookware rust and bacteria-free and reliable for a lifetime.

Seasoning

Some cast iron cookware comes pre-seasoned. If your pan is specifically labeled as pre-seasoned then you are set, but if not, then follow these simple steps:

1. Wash the pan with soap and hot water. This is important because cast iron which isn't pre-seasoned often comes with a coat of wax to protect it from rust. This should be the only time soap ever touches your pan!

2. Dry the pan thoroughly with a towel then allow the pan to completely air dry before proceeding.

3. Grease your pan all over, inside and out. I prefer to use shortening, but lard or bacon grease may also be used. Liquid oil (such as vegetable oil) is not recommended. If you find yourself in a pinch, you can use butter or Canola oil. Use a paper towel to spread a nice thin coat over the entire surface. Be careful not to miss any spot as this coating will protect your cookware from rust inside and out.

4. Heat your oven to 350° and place the pan in the oven.

5. Remove the pan from the oven after one hour. Wipe off any excess grease.

6. Allow to cool moderately.

7. Apply a fresh layer of grease and place your pan back in the oven. Let it bake for another hour.

Most cast iron manufacturers recommend you repeat this process several times to get a good sealed seasoning on your pans. The first couple of times you use the pan you should cook foods with a high fat content, such as bacon. This will help the seasoning bond to the pan. At any time should the need arise for you to use soap on your cast iron, simply re-season your pans following the steps listed above.

Wax coating on a new Dutch oven. The initial washing should be the only time soap touches your cast iron.

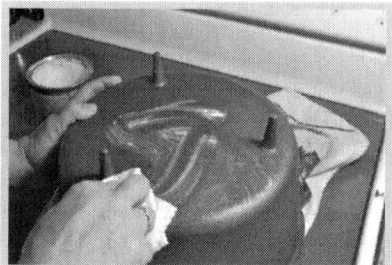

Use a paper towel to spread a nice, thin, even coat. Cover the entire pan including the legs.

Be careful not to miss any spots! Heat your pan for an hour at 350°F (176°C), then apply more grease and heat for another hour.

Cleaning

Soap should never be used to clean seasoned cast iron unless it is absolutely unavoidable, as it will break down the seasoning. Instead, while your pan is still warm, run hot water on it and scrape out any remaining food particles. I find that a steel wool pad is at times the only thing that will get food residue, although some recommend against using steel wool. The choice is yours. Another cleaning method is to boil water in the pan. This has the added benefit of killing any bacteria there might be on the pan. If soap must be used then re-season the pan.

After cleaning, make sure the pan is completely dry. Wipe it with a towel and let it air dry for a while, then add a teaspoon or two of fat or Canola oil and spread a thin layer around the pan. This not only helps keep the seasoning intact, but also is instrumental in storing the pan and preventing rust.

Storing Cast Iron

Store oiled pans uncovered in an open, dry area. If you store your pans with a lid on moisture can build up and cause the pans to rust. If your pans do rust, clean with soap and water and steel wool to remove the rust and re-season.

Homemade Equipment

While there are many pieces of cooking equipment that you may wish to purchase, it is also possible to make certain styles of ovens from scratch. It can be fun to build your own equipment, and there is a definite satisfaction in not having to spend money on expensive outdoor gear. The difficulty level can be quite low, so just about anyone who wishes to can succeed in creating perfectly functional equipment.

Cardboard Box Oven

Items required:

- Heavy-duty Cardboard Box, approx. 12"-18" each side, which opens on one side but has a flap
- Heavy Gauge Aluminum Foil
- Stapler or Glue (If you use glue, make sure that it is a type that will not soften in high heat.)
- Pen or Pencil
- Stiff Wire (Do not use plastic coated wire)
- Wire Cutters
- Metal Pie Tins
- Measuring Tape
- Charcoal
- Knife, Scissors or Awl
- Pliers (optional)

Building the oven:

1. Start by taking the cardboard box and entirely line the inside with foil, making sure that the shinier side of the foil is showing. Use a stapler to secure the foil in place. Turn the box so that the opening is facing you. The flap that opens will function as the door of your oven. It will be easiest while you are cooking if this flap is attached to the box at the side, rather than the bottom or top. The inside of the flap should also be lined with foil and secured.

2. On the left outer side of the box, measure and mark a line 4 inches from the bottom all the way across. Repeat this on the right other side of the box.

3. With your knife or scissors, punch 2 small holes about 4 inches apart into the left side of the box along the line you have just drawn. Make sure your holes extend through the foil lining inside the box.

4. Measure the height of the wholes and mark the other side of the boxed with that height. Punch holes on this side as well.

5. If you choose, you can bend one end of each piece of wire 90° into an L shape with your pliers.

6. Feed the straight ends of the wires through the holes on one side of the box and through the matching holes on the other side.

7. If you choose to you can bend the ends down with your pliers. It is not important to get the wire bent tightly against the box; the bends are just to ensure that the wires don't slip out later.

8. Now that you have your wire rack in place, take one of the metal pie tins and glue or staple it bottom-to-bottom to another pie tin. Slide it into the bottom of the box, under the wire rack. Slide the third pie tin onto the rack. Your oven is complete!

Place another pie tin upside down and under this one. Then place the charcoal in the top pan and the food on the wire racks.

All you have to do from this point is add burning charcoal into the pie tin, place the tin under the rack and add your food onto the rack making sure to close the box to retain the heat. A general guideline for this type of oven is to use 1-2 pieces of charcoal for every 100° of heat that you wish to provide. The larger your oven is, the more pieces of charcoal you may need to achieve the heat levels you desire.

The "Garbage Can Sam" Oven/Smoker

A couple of my good friends used to own a wonderfully unique and rustic floating cabin their grandfather built by hand on Lake Caligan in Washington in the early 1900's. He spent a couple of years painstakingly hauling in all the tools and supplies he needed ten miles on foot through thick forest.

"The Cabin" Photo courtesy of Carolyn Perlbachs.

Luckily, by the time my friends inherited it there were forestry roads that got us much closer than a ten mile hike to what we lovingly called "The Cabin." We would often take weekend trips up for rest, relaxation, and perhaps even a little college-aged partying. Needless to say we had some very memorable times hanging out, fishing, and zipping around in the small boat that a friend had built as an addition to the entertainment.

The interior was very simple; a table, a couple chairs, a wood stove and a metal garbage can. Mice could be a problem in such a rustic location, but rarely were. On one of our trips up to the cabin, much to our dismay we arrived to find a large number of mouse droppings scattered all around, but we quickly cleaned up, disinfected what we could, and got on with the fun.

Evening arrived and found us playing stupid college drinking games. By that time we had a lot of beer 'enhancing' our senses, so at first we shrugged it off when we started hearing things. We soon realized, though, that the sounds were quite real and were coming from the garbage can. One of us opened it up and we spotted a small mouse trapped at the bottom. We all felt sorry for the little guy and decided to set him free. Of course, we were pretty tipsy, and on a floating cabin it was quite tricky to manage. We ended up accidentally dropping the mouse, who we had dubbed "Garbage Can Sam," into the lake. Thankfully, he was able to quickly make his way to shore. It probably wasn't long before Sam made his way back into the cabin, but that night we were relieved that he was gone, and we felt really good about having giving him his freedom.

While none of this is actually relevant to the next oven idea, I love the name "Garbage Can Sam," and I wanted to share his story in this book. Rather than as a mousetrap, I think a far better use for a metal garbage can is as camp cooking equipment. A metal garbage can 20 or 30 gallon size may double as a smoker or an oven depending on how it is used. It's a fairly easy alternative to expensive store-bought equipment.

To use a can as a smoker will need a few key items. First you will need a non-galvanized steel can with a lid, then you will need a way to heat the smoker. This can be a hot plate or electrical element of some sort if you intend to use electricity or it can be charcoal. If you use charcoal, you will need a pan to burn it in. If you use a hot plate or barbeque element, you will need a pan to place the wood chips in. Next you will need a barbeque grate to place the food onto. Then you will need to use a couple of metal dowels to hold up the grate and a drill to drill the holes for the grate. Finally you should get a good thermometer to track the temperature of your smoker/oven.

Looking down inside the smoker without the coal pan, drip pan and grill grate.

To put the smoker together drill four holes in the can about ¾ up the can. If you are using a hot plate also drill a hole in the bottom of the can to run the cord through. Run the dowels through the holes drilled for the grate. Then drill a hole for the thermometer about halfway up the can and place the thermometer in the hole making sure it is secured. Next place the heating element or charcoal on the bottom of the can. If you are using charcoal you can use the same pan for the wood chips and add it to the charcoal. If you are using an electric plate you will need the pan for the chips which will sit on top of the heating element. In my old electric smoker, it wasn't necessary to soak the wood chips, but if you use charcoal you will definitely want to. When you are ready to smoke just light the charcoal, being careful to watch how much heat is coming from them or start the heating element. Place the wood chips in the charcoal or place in the pan on top of the heating element. Place the grill grate on the dowels and the meat on the grill. Cover and let smoke for the allotted time needed for your choice of meat.

You can also turn up the heat on this device and turn it into an oven. However, you will need to add more coals to increase the heat or get a good heating element that can produce enough heat for the can to cook in.

Finished smoker, it isn't pretty but it works great. This setup is with an electric heating element. This can also be used with charcoal when the element is removed.

Other Ovens

There are other oven options available too. For example, a pit oven and a solar reflector oven are some possibilities. If you are interested in trying them out, information can assuredly be found online or at your local library.

2
Fire & Heat Control

Your campfire is the center of your camp social life. It is the place where everyone gathers for warmth, camaraderie, fun, drinks and food. It is also, of course, your source of heat for cooking much if not all of your food. To ensure a fun and successful camping experience, your campfire must be handled properly.

Safety

Check before you head out to your campsite about burn bans in your area. Under certain weather conditions, campfires may be prohibited. If there is a burn ban, do not burn. Not only can there be huge fines for disregarding burn bans, but the risk of starting a forest fire is real. Lives and livelihoods are at stake.

Always build your fire in a designated fire pit. A fire pit can be as simple as a circle of rocks at the center of a cleared space. If you choose to build your own pit make sure you clear away any branches, brush, and debris surrounding your pit. Clear a wide enough area so that if anything is propelled out of the fire unexpectedly (beware the flaming marshmallow, chunk of improperly balanced firewood, or random adventurous spark) it will not land on an available fuel source. Lastly, don't build your fire under tree branches.

Never pour liquid fuel onto hot coals to try to jump start your fire for both safety and food flavor reasons. My friend Ross learned the folly of trying to do so one weekend when he, our friend Butch and I were setting up a campfire. The wind was kicking up and Ross was having trouble lighting the fire. He decided it would be a good idea to use gasoline to speed the process, so he grabbed a gas can from the truck and began pouring fuel onto the smoldering coals. In a split second, the can was on fire and Ross was madly waving it around in an attempt to extinguish the flames. Butch and I yelled at him to drop the can, which he did, and Butch swiftly kicked dirt over it to smother the flames. Fortunately the container had held very little gasoline; had the can been full, the incident could have ended quite tragically.

Be sure you completely extinguish all fire sources, including buried coals, before you leave your campsite. Coals can smolder for days under the ashes, and may be a source of secondary fires if leaves or other flammables are carried into the hot coals by animals, wind or inadvertent human action. The safest course is to pour water into your fire pit, eliminating all traces of heat.

While fire is a beautiful and useful tool, it carries inherent risks. From melted equipment to painful burns to forest fires, there are consequences to improper handling of fire. It is an unhappy camping trip that ends in a visit to the emergency room or with the destruction of wildlife and habitat. A careless moment can have life-long consequences, so it is important that you respect fire and its dangers.

How to Treat a Minor Burn

My mother was a nurse, and she always told me to run cold water over a minor burn for at least 5 minutes. If you don't have cold running water then try the cold melted water in a cooler. I recently did this after burning myself on a pie iron and it was incredibly soothing. Ice can cause further damage, and ointments, oils and butters trap heat and should not be used until the burn has completely cooled. **For anything worse than a minor burn, seek medical attention as soon as possible.** Again, The Culinary Camper accepts no liability in improper use of fire or in treating burns.

Tarps and Your Fire

Living in the Pacific Northwest we fight with the rain quite a bit. In fact, one of the types of stereotypical North westerners highlighted in the humorous advertisements of a major insurance company is the "Blue-Tarp Camper." A blue-tarp camper is a person who doesn't own anything so mollycoddling as a recreational vehicle, goes camping regardless of the weather forecast, and refuses to go home no matter how bad the weather gets. Of course this is an extreme, but one can have a lot of fun in rainy weather if one plans for it.

Different people choose to 'prepare' in different ways. My friend Darcie embraces her Native American heritage with a sense of humor. Years ago, she began a tradition of holding an 'anti-rain dance' at the start of our camping trips. We would set up camp and then dance silently around the fire pit drinking adult beverages. As this usually happened while it was sunny out, I can't really say if it worked or not... but we eventually learned that it would behoove us to bring tarps and twine on our trip just in case. Starting a fire with wet wood is miserable, and trying to keep it going and build it up is difficult and time-consuming. Bring tarps and save yourself the headache of fighting with wet fuel and keeping your body dry as well. Always make sure your tarps are clear of any fire or floating embers and you will have a much more enjoyable camp cooking experience.

Building the Fire

There are three elements to building a good cooking fire: materials with which to start the fire (including an ignition source), firewood to burn, and the coals left after the fire has died down. All of these are important for different aspects of the camp cooking process. Don't be overwhelmed though – making a fire is easy, especially with the benefits of modern chemistry.

The first thing you will need once your fire pit is prepared is tinder, small bits of material that will light easily and burn quickly. You can use dry slivers of wood, twists of dense paper, cardboard, or chemically pre-treated fire-starting sticks, which you can purchase online or most places where outdoor equipment is sold. You can even make your own fire-starters out of old cardboard egg carton sections filled with a solidified mixture of grease and paraffin. As long as it is easy to light, burns quickly, and is small enough to fit in and around your larger pieces of firewood, just about anything will work for tinder as long as it's dry and flammable.

No matter what type of tinder you use, you want it to burn long enough to light larger pieces of firewood. You should have enough to keep feeding the flames for at least several minutes. If your firewood is damp, then it will take even longer for the tinder to do its job.

Be sure your tinder stays dry – damp tinder can make your fire building experience miserable. I remember trying to build a fire in the midst of a steady drizzle during a backpacking trip to Mount Si in Western Washington. All I had for tinder was a roll of toilet paper, which sucked up moisture from the air in record time. I did finally manage to get the fire going, but it took the entire role of toilet paper to get it started. This fire would have been much easier with better preparation and proper tinder would have saved me the pain of no toilet paper for the rest of the trip.

Tinder is important, but of course you need firewood as well. You should be sure that you collect your firewood before you light the tinder. Having to go hunt for wood while your tinder is burning is a sure sign that your fire is doomed and you will have to start over. If you bring firewood from home to your campsite, covering it with a tarp is an easy way to insure that it stays dry.

Types of Campfires

Once you have your fire pit, ignition source, tinder and firewood, you're ready to start building your fire. There are many different ways to craft a fire, but I usually choose between the teepee style fire and the log cabin-style fire or some combination of both. Either of these methods will give you a good start for a cooking fire. What matters is that you build a big enough fire to give you sufficient coals with which to cook once the fire has burned down. Your fire should be at least twice as large as the equipment you will use for your meal preparation.

Make sure you have your wood prepared before building your fire.

The teepee method is a good method to use if you have lots of smaller sticks for firewood. To build a teepee fire, lay your tinder in a small bundle in the middle of the fire pit. Take a few small twigs or sticks and press them into the ground so that they angle inward and their tops cross each other just above the tinder. Make sure they are pressed deeply enough into the ground to form a stable framework.

Fill in the spaces between the stabilized sticks with sticks of a similar size, leaving a bit of an opening on one side through which you can light your tinder. Proceed to place layers of larger and larger sticks around the teepee until you have your desired fire size, always remembering to leave the opening. Once you have built your teepee to the desired size, insert your igniter into the opening and light the tinder. It should start fairly easily. Once the fire is burning nicely, you may start to add small logs leaning them on the teepee to keep building it up.

Almost ready to light but needs a few more pieces inside.

Log cabin fires are easy to craft, and are particularly useful if you have some larger pieces of firewood to use as a backdrop for the fire. For this method, you start with a pile of tinder in the middle of the fire pit, be sure to use enough tinder to get the logs around it ignited. Next, place two larger sticks or very small logs parallel to each other on either side of the tinder bundle keeping the logs close to the tinder so they ignite. After that, place two or three more small logs perpendicularly across the first two, forming a square around the tinder. Be aware that it is more difficult to leave an opening for lighting the log cabin style fire, so when you place your sticks and logs, try to ensure that there you have left space enough to success-fully insert your ignition source. Continue to add wood, alternat-ing directions, until the structure is the desired size, and then light the tinder. The tinder should catch and ignite the rest of the logs around it. After which you can start adding more wood if needed.

This is a basic log cabin fire. I start with two large logs on the bottom
and add smaller ones perpendicular to them.

Charcoal

I own a small portable camping grill. Though it isn't ideal, there are occasionally times when it isn't possible to use a campfire for cooking, and a small grill can completely replace a pit fire. I bring charcoal along in case I need it for the grill. I find that charcoal comes in handy in campfire cooking as well. Once the fire is burning well, you can add charcoal. In very short order you will have lots of extra hot coals to work with. This can be especially useful if you're using a lot of cast iron cookware. If you use charcoal treated with lighter fluid, make sure to allow the flames to die down completely and burn off the lighter fluid so it does not taint the taste of your food. Using charcoal is a great way of being efficient!

Controlling Heat

Successful camp cookery is all about heat control! Every chef, regardless of style, will say the same thing, and it is true whether you cook over a campfire or if you are in your kitchen over your stove. Of course, sometimes you don't need heat when cooking but I am only talking about cooked items. Nothing is worse than biting into a piece of meat that is dangerously raw or badly charred, and all the great marinades and spices you put on your food won't mean a thing if your food is over or under-cooked. Just as you would control the heat of a kitchen stove or gas barbeque grill, you must control the heat of your campfire. It will likely take some time to learn to gauge your heat just right, but don't be afraid to practice and don't be afraid to mess up – that is one way to learn.

There are three main types of heat for the cook to utilize from a campfire: flames, coals, and reflected heat. To achieve all three, once you have a good-sized fire going nicely let the wood burn down for about an hour. This will form a good base of coals. From this point on you must watch how much wood goes into the fire.

Keep your pyromaniac friends and family at bay until the cooking is done! Once you begin cooking, you will need to maintain your heat levels by judiciously adding wood or charcoal to the fire. A third heat type you can use is indirect heat. Indirect heat is excellent for slow cooking barbequed food such as ribs. Indirect heat can be difficult to manage but if you can manipulate the campfire area to utilize this type of heat you can produce some very tasty smoked foods.

The placement of wood and foods into the fire pit is a bit of a balancing act, as some foods cook more quickly than others. Direct coals and flames will create a good searing heat and will heat food very quickly. When you are using the bed of coals to cook a dish, at times you will find it beneficial to add wood. You don't want to add so much wood that it flares and burns everything around it. Instead, add it to the fire at a distance slightly removed from your food. This will help keep coals alive without the intense heat of direct flame enveloping your dish. For more slowly cooked foods, such as ribs or pork shoulder, you may want to use indirect heat to achieve the low and slow cooking method implemented by many barbecue enthusiasts. To do this you will place the food into the fire pit near, but completely removed from the coals. Be aware that it will take much longer for food to cook using this method, and when in doubt use a meat thermometer to ensure that your meat is thoroughly cooked. It may take some practice to perfect using the different heat types successfully, but the delicious food will make it all worth the effort.

How hot is that fire?

There are a few ways you can judge the cooking heat of your fire, but all of them demand you use extreme caution doing so. One is to use a quick-acting oven thermometer and carefully hold the thermometer over the heat to check the temperature. If you choose this method you can use the following temperatures as a cooking guide. *All temperatures in *The Culinary Camper* are listed in Fahrenheit.*

225°-250° = Low
250°-325° = Low-Medium
325°-375° = Medium
375°-450° = Medium-High
450°-600° = High

I prefer to use the hand method. This involves holding your hand over the coals and counting the seconds until you can't stand the heat any longer. Use extreme caution using this method. Here is a good guide to judging heat with your hand over a fire or coals.

Low: 11-15 seconds. This is called the low and slow method. This is the one true method for the pure barbecue enthusiast. It can be difficult to manipulate the fire environment enough to maintain a consistent low heat for hours, but it is possible with practice and ingenuity.

Medium Low: 8-10 seconds over the heat. This is a good range for reheating foods but is not a good browning temperature.

Medium: 6-7 seconds over the heat. This a good heat for more gradual cooking methods; it will brown slowly while cooking meat thoroughly throughout. It is a great temp for cooking chickens, turkey and roasts. If you have some sort of cover, you can maintain this heat for up to 60 minutes without having to fiddle with your fire too much.

Medium High: 4-5 seconds over the heat. This is a great range for searing and grilling with direct heat. It only takes about 5 to 10 minutes to go from high to medium heat when you spread out your coals. This temperature will generally last about 10 to 15 minutes without cover.

High: 1 second over the heat. If you can only hold your hand over the heat for about 1 second, your fire is probably too hot to cook most food, but will be great for burning debris off your grill and cleaning it.

Of course, if you are extremely under- or over-sensitive to heat you will need to adapt the guide to your needs or use a thermometer to help you judge the heat.

Controlling Heat: Dutch Oven Cooking

Dutch ovens are thick-walled cooking pots with tightly fitting lids, usually made of cast iron. Dutch oven cooking is an art form many people take extremely seriously. There are Dutch oven clubs and competitions all around the world; the International Dutch Oven Society is a non-profit based in Utah, and is a wonderful resource if you are interested in learning more about Dutch oven cookery.

Cooking over an open fire or with charcoal can be challenging because many recipes call for a specific temperature. Luckily there are ways to calculate the amount of heat you get from coals when cooking with a Dutch oven. Dutch ovens are extremely useful for campfire cooking because they can be put directly into the coals without taking damage. In addition, many Dutch ovens have slightly concave lids, enabling coals to be placed on top to ensure more even cooking.

The amount of coals is more than in previously mentioned ovens because of the thickness of the pots and because the coals are in direct external contact with the iron which radiates the heat to the inside and cooks the food.

Use the following chart to determine the approximate amount of coals you will need for your recipes.

10" DUTCH OVEN

325° - 19 coals ....OR............. 13 on top / 6 on bottom
350° - 21 coals ....OR............. 14 on top / 7 on bottom
375° - 23 coals ....OR............. 16 on top / 7 on bottom
400° - 25 coals ....OR............. 17 on top / 8 on bottom
425° - 27 coals ....OR............. 18 on top / 9 on bottom
450° - 29 coals ....OR............. 19 on top / 10 on bottom

12" DUTCH OVEN

325° - 23 coals ....OR............. 16 on top / 7 on bottom

350° - 25 coals ....OR............. 17 on top / 8 on bottom
375° - 27 coals ....OR............. 18 on top / 9 on bottom
400° - 29 coals ....OR............. 19 on top / 10 on bottom
425° - 31 coals ....OR............. 21 on top / 10 on bottom
450° - 33 coals ....OR............. 22 on top / 11 on bottom

14" DUTCH OVEN

325° - 30 coals ....OR............. 20 on top / 10 on bottom
350° - 32 coals ....OR............. 21 on top / 11 on bottom
375° - 34 coals ....OR............. 22 on top / 12 on bottom
400° - 36 coals ....OR............. 24 on top / 12 on bottom
425° - 38 coals ....OR............. 25 on top / 13 on bottom
450° - 40 coals ....OR............. 26 on top / 14 on bottom

Rule of thumb: Every 2 briquettes add about 25°. For larger or smaller ovens than listed you can add or remove coals as needed by using this rule.

Notice the chart shows more coals on top, this is because the bottom of the pot is touching the food directly while the top has a layer of air separating it. By putting more coals on top you can heat that layer more efficiently. This is ideal for baking so if you need to boil foods or fry them, putting more coals on the bottom may be a better method.

Ideally, charcoal is placed in a ring on the top and bottom of the Dutch oven to distribute heat as evenly as possible. The chef can manipulate either the lid or the entire oven to move the heat around if necessary. Placement of the coals should be either in a solid circle or spaced 1- 2 inches apart. For higher temperatures, the solid line works well; for a lower temp you might want to space them out more.

For longer cooking times it will be necessary to change dying coals for fresh ones partway through. This can be done by placing fresh unlit briquettes so that they touch the hot ones on and underneath your Dutch oven; they will kindle and be hot by the time the first ones die down. Alternately, have another complete batch hot and ready to switch to after about an hour depending on how fast your coals burn.

3

Brines, Gravies, Rubs, Marinades, Sauces, and Seasonings

Sauces and seasonings are what make food taste good, they are meant to enhance the natural flavor of the food. You could cook without any spices, but your food would get boring very quickly. This chapter of *The Culinary Camper* focuses on these wonderful, flavorful accompaniments, which will be used in many of the recipes in the following chapters. Many can be made well ahead of your camping trip; some sauces like barbeque sauce are actually better when they have been allowed to 'rest' in the fridge and let the spices blend. Whether you make them at home and bring them in a travel container or make them on site, they will make your campground cooking smell fantastic and taste even better.

Alfredo Sauce

Alfredo sauce is a creamy garlicky sauce that is traditionally ladled over noodles and is wonderful served with chicken, shrimp and other seafood.

Equipment

Saucepan (or Dutch Oven)
Wire Whisk

Ingredients

¼ c. butter
1 c. cream
1-2 cloves garlic
(peeled)
1 c. parmesan cheese
½ tsp. basil
½ tsp. oregano
1 tsp. parsley
½ tsp. salt and pepper
(or to taste)

Steps

Melt butter in a saucepan over medium heat and add cream and slowly simmer for 5 minutes. Add garlic and cheese and whisk quickly, until cheese is blended. Stir in basil, oregano, parsley, salt and pepper, and serve with pasta or over chicken. I like to add mushrooms to my sauce but that is purely optional.

❖   ❖   ❖   ❖

"BobbiQue Sauce"

I'm notorious for bringing barbeque sauce camping with me. There is something about campfire cooking with barbeque sauce that I just love, maybe because flavors seem so much smokier cooked over a fire that it just fits. An old friend once said that I was so addicted to barbeque sauce that it should be called "BobbiQue Sauce," this name sticks to this day.

BobbiQue Sauce (Classic Carolina Style)

This is my favorite style of barbeque sauce and works especially well with pork dishes.

Equipment

Saucepan (or Dutch Oven)
Wire Whisk (or Cooking Spoon)

Ingredients

2 c. cider vinegar
2 tbsp. molasses
1 tbsp. ground dry mustard
1/2 c. butter
1/4 tsp. cayenne pepper
1 tbsp. Worcestershire
1 c. dark brown sugar
   (firmly packed)
4 tsp. cornstarch
1 c. water (cold)

Steps

In a saucepan, mix cider vinegar, molasses, dry mustard, butter, cayenne pepper, Worcestershire and brown sugar over medium heat. Bring to a boil. In a cup, mix cornstarch thoroughly with water. Slowly pour the cornstarch mixture into the saucepan, stirring continually. Bring sauce back up to a simmer and remove from heat. Serve with your favorite barbecued pork, chicken or beef.

BobbiQue Sauce (Classic Texas Style)

This sauce works really well with chicken and beef dishes but still tastes good on pork as well. I came up with this recipe after a couple of visits to family in Texas and fell in love with the barbeque sauce.

Equipment

Saucepan
  (or Dutch Oven)
Cooking Spoon

Ingredients

2 cans tomato paste
1 c. dark beer
3/4 c. brown sugar
2 tbsp. honey
½ c. apple cider vinegar
½ c. water
1/4 c. olive oil
3 tsp. garlic powder
2 tbsp. Worcestershire sauce
1/2 tsp. cayenne pepper
1 tsp. paprika
1 tsp. onion powder
1 ½ tbsp. yellow mustard (or
½ tbsp. ground dried mustard)
1 tsp. liquid smoke
1/2 jalapeño minced
4 shakes ground Ghost pepper (caution, this is very hot and should be used with caution. Wear gloves when handling)

Steps

Stir ingredients together in saucepan over medium heat until sauce begins to simmer. Move to low heat. Cook for another 35 minutes, stirring occasionally, and serve with chicken, pork or beef.

❖ ❖ ❖ ❖

Brine

Brining is a method of soaking meats in a salt bath prior to cooking. It adds flavor and helps meats stay moist and tender and can help preserve meats for smoking. Brining is a great method to start at home and bring the brined meat to cook at camp.

Brine (Fish)

Equipment

1 Large Container
(able to hold at least a
gallon of liquid)
Cooking Spoon
Sealable Plastic Bags
(or Plastic Food Storage
Containers)
Ladle
Cooler
Ice

Ingredients

1 gallon water
1 c. brine salt
1 c. brown sugar (firmly
packed)
1 tsp. ground black pepper
3 tbsp. seafood seasoning
3 tsp. garlic powder or 3 tbsp.
minced garlic
1 dash lemon juice
3 tsp. onion powder
1 dash pepper sauce

Steps

Place all ingredients into large container, stirring until fully dissolved. Place fish into sealable bags or containers and ladle in brine, then seal tightly. Place sealed bags/containers into cooler and pack cooler with ice. For grilling, soak fish in brine for 30 minutes to an hour. For smoking, soak fish for 6 to 8 hours.

Brine (Pork)

Equipment

1 Large Container
(able to hold at least a
gallon of liquid)
Cooking Spoon
Plastic Sealable Bags
(or Plastic Food Storage
Containers)
Ladle
Cooler
Ice

Ingredients

2 c. apple cider vinegar
1 c. brining salt
½ c. brown sugar
1 tbsp. mustard (or mustard
powder)
3 c. water

Steps

Place all ingredients into large container, stirring until fully dissolved. Place pork into sealable bags or containers and ladle in brine, then seal tightly. Place sealed bags/containers into cooler and pack cooler with ice. Soak pork in brine for a minimum of 30 minutes, up to several hours. Brining is great for pork chops and roasts.

Brine (Poultry)

Equipment

1 Large Container
(able to hold at least 1.5
gallons of liquid)
Plastic Sealable Bags
(or Plastic Food Storage
Containers)
Ladle
Cooler & Ice

Ingredients

1 gallon water
1 c. brining salt
3 tsp. garlic powder
1 tbsp. black pepper
¼ c. brown sugar

Steps

Place all ingredients into large container, stirring until fully dissolved. Place poultry into sealable bags or containers and ladle in brine, then seal tightly. Place sealed bags/containers into cooler and pack cooler with ice. Soak for about 6 to 8 hours. Double all ingredients for turkey brine.

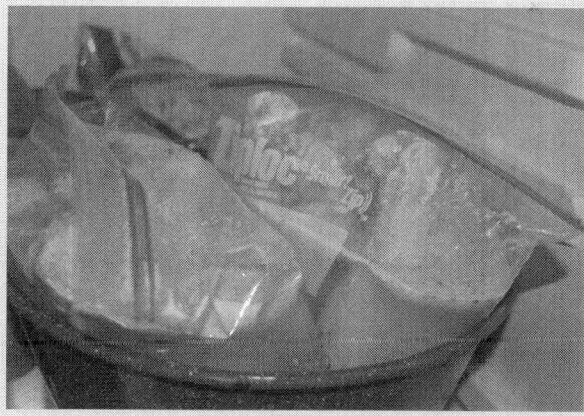

I started these chickens at home and soaked them overnight. I made them the following day.

❖   ❖   ❖   ❖

Melted Garlic Butter
(for dipping)

Equipment

Garlic Press
Saucepan
(or Dutch Oven)
Wire Whisk
(or Cooking Spoon)

Ingredients

½ stick butter
(per desired serving)
1 or 2 cloves garlic
(per desired serving)

Steps

Peel garlic and crush with garlic press. Place butter and garlic into a saucepan over low heat. Stir until butter is melted. Serve with shellfish or drizzle onto warm bread.

Herbed Butter

Equipment

Cooking Spoon
Bowl

Ingredients

½ stick butter
(room temperature)
1 clove garlic (crushed) or
powdered garlic
½ tsp. basil
½ tsp. oregano

Steps

Place all ingredients into a bowl and stir with a fork until butter is softened and ingredients are well blended.

❖   ❖   ❖   ❖

Gravy
Creamy Chicken Gravy

Equipment

Saucepan
(or Dutch Oven, or you
can use the pan in which
your meat was cooked)
Wire Whisk
(or Cooking Spoon)

Ingredients

3 tbsp. flour
3 tbsp. butter
2 c. chicken, beef or pork
broth (or pan drippings)

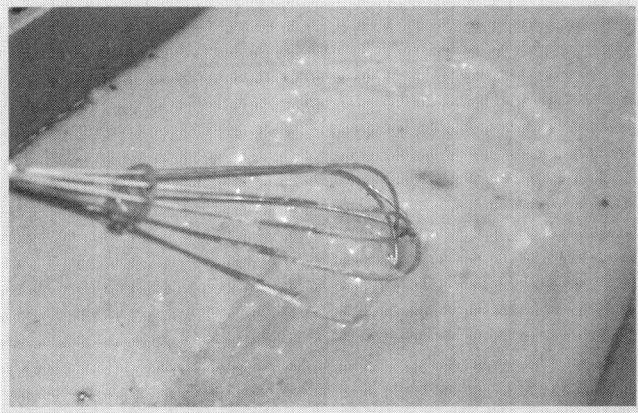

Steps

Mix together equal parts of butter and flour thoroughly in a saucepan for about 3 minutes until the flour is creamy and evenly distributed. If you are using the drippings from your meat only add enough fat as is need to equal the flour amount used. Over medium heat, slowly mix in broth, stirring until mixture reaches a very slow boil. Boil for about 10 minutes, stirring frequently until gravy reaches the desired consistency. If the gravy is too thin you can add a thickener if needed.

Gravy (Country-Style)

Equipment

Saucepan
(or Dutch Oven, or you
can use the pan in which
your meat was cooked)
Wire Whisk

Ingredients

3 tbsp. flour
3 tbsp. butter
1½ c. chicken broth or
drippings
½ c. cream (or milk)

Steps

Mix together the butter and flour thoroughly in a saucepan for about 3 minutes until the flour is creamy and evenly distributed. If you are using the drippings from your meat only add enough fat as is need to equal the flour amount used. Over medium heat, slowly mix in broth, stirring until mixture reaches a very slow boil. Boil for about 10 minutes, stirring frequently. Add cream or milk and cook for another 2 minutes or until gravy reaches the desired consistency. Add salt and pepper to taste.

❖ ❖ ❖ ❖

Guacamole

This is an easy dish to make while camping and goes great with my enchiladas.

Equipment

Medium to Large Bowl
Knife
Fork
Cutting board

Ingredients

4 ripe avocados
1 clove garlic
1 ripe tomato
(seeds removed if desired)
¼ c. cilantro
¼ c. green onion
1 jalapeño finely chopped
(seeds removed if desired,
optional)
1 Chile pepper (optional)
½ fresh lime squeezed
salt and pepper (to taste)

Steps

Scoop out the avocados into the bowl, discarding pits. Peel and mince garlic clove and add to bowl. Finely chop tomato, cilantro, onion, jalapeño, and Chile pepper and add to bowl. Add lime juice, salt and pepper, and mix well. Serve chilled with chips and salsa or any Mexican style dish.

❖   ❖   ❖   ❖

Balsamic Reduction

Equipment

Saucepan
Spoon

Ingredients

2 c. balsamic vinegar
¼ c. honey
1 clove garlic
½ tsp. basil

Steps

Add the balsamic, honey and basil to a sauce pan. Smash the garlic and add it to the sauce pan. Simmer until the volume is reduced by half. Serve as a drizzle on chicken or use a small amount as a marinade or salad dressing.

❖   ❖   ❖   ❖

Piccata Sauce

Equipment

Knife
Cutting Board
Saucepan (or Dutch Oven)
Wire Whisk (or Fork)

Ingredients

3 artichoke hearts
1 c. chicken broth
1 tbsp. minced garlic
2 tbsp. lemon juice
2 tbsp. capers
½ tsp. salt
½ tsp. pepper (optional)
3 tbsp. butter
1 tbsp. cornstarch

Steps

Slice artichoke hearts into thin pieces and set aside. Put broth and garlic into saucepan and bring to a boil over high heat. Lower heat until the boiling has slowed to a simmer then stir in artichokes, lemon juice, capers, salt and pepper. Simmer for another 3 or 4 minutes. Add butter and stir until fully melted, then whisk cornstarch in a ¼ cup of water and stir in, stir continually until the sauce has reached the desired consistency.

❖　❖　❖　❖

Italian Style Red Meat Sauce

Equipment

Knife
Cutting Board
Skillet
Saucepan (or Dutch Oven)
Cooking Spoon

Ingredients

½ onion
4 cloves garlic
1 lb ground beef (any other ground meats may be substituted, though you may need to add 2 tbsp. olive oil if you use turkey, which tends to be more dry.)
3 cans tomato sauce
1 can stewed tomatoes
2 cans tomato paste
2 tbsp. oregano
2 tbsp. basil
(optional: chopped bell peppers, sliced mushrooms, shredded carrots)
parmesan cheese (to taste)

Steps

Peel and chop garlic and onion and set aside. Brown the meat in the frying pan, drain the grease, and add the meat to a saucepan or Dutch oven. Stir in tomato sauce, stewed tomatoes, tomato paste, garlic, oregano and basil. Bring to a simmer over medium heat. Simmer for about 45 minutes, add onion and any other optional ingredients. Simmer for another 35 minutes. Serve with noodles and top with parmesan cheese. This sauce is also good to use in Lasagna.

Simply omit meat from the recipe for a vegetarian Marinara sauce.

❖   ❖   ❖   ❖

Rubs

Rub (Beef)

Equipment

Spoon
Mixing Bowl
Glass Jar with Lid
(or Sealable Food
Storage Container)

Ingredients

2 tbsp. brown sugar
4 tbsp. mustard powder
4 tbsp. paprika
4 tbsp. garlic
2 tsp. basil

2 tsp. oregano
1 tsp. savory
1 tsp. thyme
1 ½ tsp. pepper
1 tbsp. kosher salt

Steps

Mix together and store in sealed container in a cool, dark, dry place.

Rub (Blackened Seasoning)

Equipment

Spoon
Mixing Bowl
Glass Jar with Lid
(or Sealable Food Storage
Container)

Ingredients

4 tsp. paprika
6 tsp. dried ground Chile pepper
4 tsp. onion powder
4 tsp. garlic powder
2 tbsp. brown sugar
4 tsp. kosher salt
4 tsp. pepper
3 tsp. cayenne pepper
2 tsp. ground cumin
1 tsp. basil
1 tsp. oregano

Steps

Mix together and store in sealed container in a cool, dark, dry place.

Rub (Poultry)

Equipment

Spoon
Mixing Bowl
Glass Jar with Lid
(or Sealable Food Storage
Container)

Ingredients

2 tbsp. pepper
2 tbsp. brown sugar
4 tsp. cayenne pepper
4 tbsp. Chili powder
2 tbsp. cumin
3 tbsp. garlic powder
1 tbsp. oregano
1 tbsp. basil
6 tbsp. paprika
1 tbsp. mustard powder
2 tbsp. salt

Steps

Mix together and store in sealed container in a cool, dark, dry place.

Rub (Pork)

Equipment

Spoon
Mixing Bowl
Glass Jar with Lid
(or Sealable Food Storage
Container)

Ingredients

5 tbsp. brown sugar
1 tsp. basil
1 tsp. oregano
4 tsp. garlic powder
4 tsp. Chili powder
1 tsp. cayenne pepper
1 tsp. black pepper
1 tsp. salt
1 tsp. mustard powder
1 tsp. sage (optional)

Steps

Mix together and store in sealed container in a cool, dark, dry place.

Pork Rub Prior to Stirring

Pork Rub (Mixed)

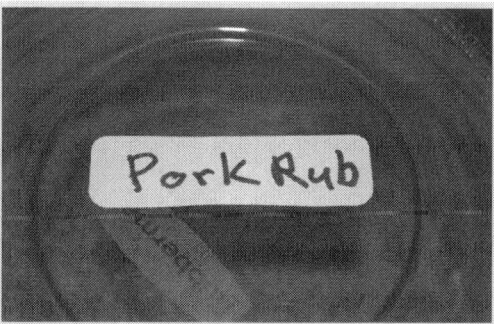

Be sure you label your storage containers.

❖   ❖   ❖   ❖

Chunky Salsa

Equipment

Large Bowl
Knife
Cutting board

Ingredients

2 large tomatoes
(remove seeds if desired)
2 garlic cloves
2 green chilies
(or 5 oz. canned green chilies)
2 Jalapeños
(remove seeds if desired)
3 green onions
½ c. fresh cilantro
juice of 1 fresh lime
1 tsp. salt
1 tsp. pepper
1 tsp. ground cumin
1 tbsp. olive oil

Steps

For a chunky salsa, finely dice the tomatoes, garlic, chilies and jalapeños. Chop the green onions down to about ¼ inch and coarsely chop the cilantro. Combine all ingredients in the bowl. Add a little water if the salsa is too thick. Stir well and refrigerate for an hour before serving.

❖   ❖   ❖   ❖

Taco Sauce

Equipment

Mixing Bowl
Spoon
Knife
Cutting Board
Cooler
Ice

Ingredients

½ c. mayonnaise
½ c. plain yogurt
juice of 1 lime
½ tsp. garlic powder
1 tsp. chipotle hot sauce

Steps

Thoroughly mix mayonnaise and yogurt in a bowl. Squeeze in the juice of 1 lime and add the garlic powder and hot sauce. Stir all the ingredients together and chill while you make your tacos.

❖ ❖ ❖ ❖

VK's Teriyaki Sauce

My friend Butch likes to make this at home and marinade thin beef slices in a plastic container which he then brings camping to make on a stick over a campfire. This is a very yummy sauce.

Equipment

Sauce Pan
Spoon or Wire Whisk

Ingredients

1 c. soy sauce
1 c. sugar (white, brown, raw)
use less honey or molasses
1 c. stock
1 c. water
1 tsp. onion powder
1 tsp. ginger
1 tsp. garlic
1 tsp. red pepper flakes or
Chili powder

Steps

Heat all ingredients till just boiling stirring often. Place in container, let cool and refrigerate. It will keep for 4 weeks. To thicken use a tablespoon of corn starch and use as a dipping sauce. This is an excellent marinade for beef jerky as well.

❖   ❖   ❖   ❖

Kalbe Marinade

Like Teriyaki this is great to make at home and start your marinade for your favorite meats.

Equipment

Mixing bowl
Wire Wisk

Ingredients

2/3 c. soy sauce
3 tbsp. water
3 tbsp. honey
3 tbsp. molasses
2 tbsp. sesame oil
2 garlic cloves, crushed
½ tsp. red pepper
2 tbsp. finely chopped green onion
1 tbsp. toasted sesame seeds

Steps

Combine all ingredients and mix well and refrigerate. Add meat for at least 30 minutes for marinade.

❖   ❖   ❖   ❖

4

Salads, Appetisers and Side Dishes

Seasoned French Fries

Equipment

Dutch Oven
Potato Peeler
(optional)
Knife
Cutting Board
Mixing Bowl
Cooking Spoon

Slotted Metal Spatula
(or Wire "Bird's Nest"
Basket)
Paper Towels
Candy Deep Frying
Thermometer

Ingredients

1 qt. peanut oil
(or canola oil)
6 large potatoes
1 tsp. garlic salt
1 tsp. salt
1 tsp. paprika
1 tsp. Chili powder

Steps

This is a good recipe to make on a camp or RV stove because you need to maintain a high temperature long enough to cook the fries. Heat up the oil to 350°. While the oil is heating, peel potatoes. If desired, leave the skins on for flavor and texture. Slice potatoes into thin strips about 1/8 to 1/16 inch thick. Mix seasonings together and set aside. With a paper towel, dry the potatoes by dabbing them with the towel. Place chips in the hot oil. Once the potatoes start to brown, remove them from the oil. Drain on a paper towel, sprinkle with seasoning mix and serve.

Aunt Polly's Awesome Baked Beans

Besides being a really awesome person, my Aunt Polly was one of the most amazing cooks I have ever known. One summer when we were visiting family in Minnesota, Aunt Polly made this dish for a family re-union and we couldn't get enough of it. Avid recipe collector that my mother was, she refused to leave without Polly's recipe for baked beans. I just hope that I'm not disclosing some ancient family secret from Polly's side of the family, because I'm passing it on to you. These baked beans are an amazing combination of slow cooked beans, bacon and spices that will make your mouth water just thinking about them.

Equipment

Cutting Board
Knife
Dutch Oven (with Lid)
Skillet
Spoon

Ingredients

2 Lbs. navy beans (dried)
¾ - ½ lb. bacon
1 onion (small)
2 tsp. salt
4 tbsp. molasses
1 - 1 ½ c. brown sugar
2 -3 tsp. dry mustard
8 - 10 c. water
½ c. ketchup
½ tsp. black pepper

Steps

Rinse and soak beans if necessary. Peel and chop onion; chop bacon. Cook bacon in the skillet until just barely beginning to crisp. Add the onions and continue to cook until the onions have begun to turn translucent. Drain the grease and transfer bacon and onion, plus the remaining ingredients, to the Dutch oven. Cover and simmer all ingredients together, stirring occasionally, for 8 to 10 hours over low heat around 225° using 15 coals with 9 on top and 6 on bottom. If you cook at a higher temperature the beans will be done sooner so check them for doneness.

❖ ❖ ❖ ❖

Beer Cheese Soup

Equipment

Dutch Oven
(or Stock Pot)
Cooking Spoon

Ingredients

2 cans condensed cream of mushroom soup
1 can condensed cream of broccoli soup
1 tsp. Worcestershire sauce
2 cans beer
½ lb. grated cheddar cheese
¼ lb. grated pepper jack cheese
¼ tsp. garlic powder

Steps

Over low-medium heat, combine condensed soups, beer and Worcestershire sauce in a Dutch oven or large pan and stir well. Once the liquid is beginning to simmer, slowly add the cheeses and stir them into the soup until melted. Simmer slowly for about 20 minutes, stirring occasionally; lower heat levels if necessary so the soup does not scorch. Serve with bread sticks or French bread.

Caprese Salad

Equipment

Knife
Cutting Board
Plate (or Bowl)
Cup
Fork

Ingredients

1 log fresh mozzarella
(or 1 pkg. mozzarella balls)
1-2 tomatoes (medium or large)
fresh basil
1 tbsp. olive oil
1 tbsp. balsamic vinegar

Steps

Slice tomato into ¼ inch of smaller slices. Lay slices out on a plate. Slice mozzarella log into ¼ inch or smaller slices and place mozzarella onto tomato slices. Chop basil and sprinkle over slices. Drizzle balsamic vinegar over tomato/mozzarella stacks then drizzle with oil; serve promptly.

If using mozzarella balls: Cut tomato into large chunks. Chop basil. Toss all ingredients into bowl and mix well to make an excellent salad.

❖   ❖   ❖   ❖

Corn on the Cob

This is an incredibly simple recipe and one of my favorite ways to cook corn on the cob.

Equipment

Fire Grate
(or Aluminum Foil)
Oven Mitts
(or other hand protection)

Ingredients

2 to 4 ears corn (still in husks)
2 tbsp. butter
salt (or flavored salt)
Seasonings (optional)

Steps

Place the ears, still in their husks, onto the grate directly over the fire at a medium to medium high heat. Turn the corn a quarter turn every 5 minutes to ensure even cooking. After about 20 minutes remove from the heat, using oven mitts and peel off husks. Rub with butter and add salt and seasonings as desired.

If you do not have a fire grate, wrap the ears in foil and put them directly into the coals. This is a trickier method, so turn the ears frequently and check to make sure they aren't burning. I've seen some people toss the cobs directly into the fire without the foil.

❖   ❖   ❖   ❖

Mac and Cheese

This is one of my top ten comfort foods. Usually people throw it together using a boxed mix made with powdered 'cheese,' but this is a much tastier way to make it, and you know for sure that the cheese is real when you add it yourself. You can't beat this cheesy baked noodle goodness.

Equipment

Dutch Oven
Cooking Spoon
Colander
Wire Whisk

Ingredients

2 qt. water
4 c. dried elbow macaroni
½ c. butter (1 stick)
½ c. flour
3 c. milk
(or cream if you want to be really decadent!)
1½ lb. grated cheddar cheese
1 tsp. salt

1 tsp. pepper
½-1 lb. pre-cooked ground beef (or try ground buffalo meat instead for an exotic addition.)
garlic breadcrumbs (optional)
½ c. grated parmesan cheese

Mac and Cheese with mushrooms

Steps

Over high heat, bring 2 qt. water to boil in a large pan. Add elbow macaroni and cook, stirring occasionally, to just barely al dente; set aside in the colander to drain. Place your pan back over medium-low heat and melt the butter. When butter is completely melted, slowly whisk in flour and cook for 3 minutes, add salt and pepper. Add milk and continue whisking until the mixture is smooth. As the milk heats, add the cheddar cheese bit by bit, stirring continually so that the cheese melts into the sauce without sticking or clumping. (You can reserve a bit of the cheddar cheese to sprinkle on top if you like a cheesy crust.) Once all the cheese is melted, add the cooked noodles and stir until macaroni is thoroughly mixed in. If you choose to add pre-cooked ground meat or mushrooms, add it at this time. Remove from heat; top with breadcrumbs and Parmesan cheese and any reserved cheese. Cover, and bake at 350° using 25 coals with 17 on top and 8 on bottom. Cook for about 30 minutes. Remove lid and let stand for a few minutes to cool before serving.

❖　❖　❖　❖

Macaroni Salad

This is a good recipe to prep all or part of at home and bring to the campsite in the cooler packed on ice. Since Macaroni Salad is always best the next day I prefer to make this at home and bring it along in the cooler. It stores nicely in freezer bags.

Equipment

Dutch Oven
(or large
Saucepan)
Colander
Large Mixing
Bowl
Spoon
Cooler & Ice

Ingredients

½ gal. water
3 c. macaroni noodles
1 tbsp. salt
1 clove garlic (minced)
3 eggs (hard-boiled, chopped)
1 ½ c. mayonnaise
1 c. celery (chopped)
1/8 c. green bell pepper (diced)
1/8 c. red bell pepper (diced)
1/8 c. yellow bell pepper (diced)

¼ c. green onion (chopped)
¼ c. onion (chopped)
1 tbsp. basil
1 tbsp. oregano
1 tbsp. parsley
3 tbsp. yellow mustard
1/8 c. capers (optional)
½ c. shrimp, chicken, turkey, fresh tuna, smoked salmon (optional)
1 egg (hard-boiled, sliced; optional)

Steps

Bring water to a boil in a Dutch oven or large sauce pan, reserve some water to cool the noodles after cooking. When water is boiling, add macaroni noodles. Cook until noodles are al dente. (Do not allow the noodles to overcook or become mushy.) While noodles are cooking, combine all remaining ingredients (except the reserved water) in the large mixing bowl.

Remove noodles from heat, drain, and rinse with the remaining cool water. Drain again. Once the noodles are drained and cool, add them to the mixture in the mixing bowl and stir gently until thoroughly mixed. Place salad in cooler with ice to chill for at least 2 hours prior to serving. Garnish with fresh parsley and/or sliced hard-boiled egg. This salad is even better the next day once all the ingredients have had a chance to meld together.

❖ ❖ ❖ ❖

Mashed Potatoes

Equipment

Dutch oven or large pot
Potato Peeler (optional)
Knife
Cutting Board
Colander
Fork
Potato Masher

Ingredients

10 Yukon gold potatoes
water
4-6 cloves garlic (peeled)
1 tsp. salt
1 stick butter
1-2 c. milk (or cream)
3 tbsp. capers (optional, but highly recommended)
salt and pepper (to taste)

Steps

Wash the potatoes and peel them if desired. Quarter the potatoes and place them in the Dutch oven or large pot. Add enough water to cover all the potatoes. Add the peeled garlic and salt to the water. Cover the pot and put on high heat and bring to a boil. After 15 minutes at a low boil, check the potatoes, and then every couple minutes after that. Poke them with a fork to see if they are soft clear through. Be sure not to leave them too long or they will start to disintegrate. Drain the water with a colander and place the potatoes and garlic back into the pot. Add the butter and begin mashing the potatoes. Once the butter has melted add the cup of milk or cream and mix thoroughly. If the potatoes reach a smooth, thick consistency then they are probably ready; if they seem dry add a little more milk. It is better to start with too little liquid and add a bit more than to start with too much and have soupy potatoes.

Once the potatoes are mashed to the desired consistency, add the capers, salt and pepper to taste, and serve. The capers add a nice salty zing, and in my opinion this recipe makes the best darn mashed potatoes in the world.

❖   ❖   ❖   ❖

Nana Tidwell's Curried Pea Salad

Equipment

Knife
Cutting Board
Mixing Bowl
Spoon

Ingredients

2 bunches scallions
1 6 oz can smoked almonds
2 lbs. frozen peas
1 ½ c. mayonnaise
2 tsp. curry powder

Steps

Chop scallions and almonds. Let peas thaw slightly; they should still be somewhat icy. In a mixing bowl, add together all ingredients and stir well. Place in a cooler to rest for about an hour. Serve cold.

❖　❖　❖　❖

Ole Man Tidwell's Stuffed Tomato Salad

This was my father's recipe. He liked to serve it for holidays and it was very good.

Equipment

Knife
Cutting Board
Small Mixing Bowl
Spoon
Dish (or shallow Bowl)

Ingredients

2 avocados
1 tsp. seafood seasoning
1 c. bay shrimp (pre-cooked)
4 ripe tomatoes (whole, round)
2-3 tbsp. Italian dressing

Steps

Scoop out the avocados (discarding peel and seed) slice each half into quarters. Place shrimp into the mixing bowl and blend well with seafood seasoning. Set aside. Using the knife, make 4 or 5 cuts down the center of the non-stemmed side of each tomato until just before you reach the bottom stem side, remove inner core and seeds if desired. The tomatoes should open into a star pattern. Spoon the shrimp mixture onto the tomatoes and gently place avocado slices onto the shrimp and sprinkle with the Italian dressing. Serve cold.

❖   ❖   ❖   ❖

Roasted Artichokes

Equipment

Cutting Board
Sharp Knife
Aluminum Foil
Small Sauce Pan
Fire Grate
(or Grill)

Oven Mitts (or other
hand protection)
Plate
Bowl
(or garbage bag)

Ingredients

1 artichoke
1 tbsp. olive oil
1 stick butter
(or mayonnaise)

Steps

Place butter in sauce pan and set near fire or on stove to melt.

On a flat surface, place a piece of aluminum foil large enough to completely wrap around the

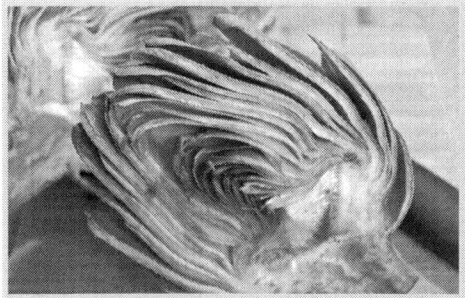

artichoke. Prepare a second piece of foil the same size so you can wrap it twice for better cooking results.

With the knife, cut the Artichoke in half lengthwise and sprinkle a little olive oil all around each piece. Sprinkle with salt and pepper if desired. Place artichoke half cut side down onto the foil and wrap the aluminum foil completely around the artichoke with the first piece of foil. Wrap again with the second piece of foil. Seal the open ends by pinching and rolling foil. Repeat for second artichoke half.

Place artichoke halves on a grate over a medium hot fire for about 30 to 45 minutes or in coals checking for doneness after 30 minutes. Wearing hand protection, remove halves from fire and unwrap onto plate. Serve with melted butter or mayo.

Roasted Potatoes

Equipment

Water
Vegetable Brush (optional)
Towel
Aluminum Foil
Tongs
Oven Mitts (or Leather Gloves)

Ingredients

4-6 russet potatoes, Yukon or
Sweet potatoes
1 tbsp. olive oil
1 tsp. salt (or garlic salt)
½ tsp. pepper (optional)

Dutch oven roasted potatoes.

Steps

On a flat surface, place a piece of foil large enough to wrap completely around the potato. Wash and dry the potato, rub it with olive oil, then sprinkle it with salt (and pepper if desired.)

Set the potato in the middle of the foil, and wrap the foil around the potato. Tear off a second piece of foil and wrap it again. The double wrapping helps to prevent the skin from burning. (This recipe may be expanded to as many potatoes as will fit into the coals; repeat all of these steps until each potato is wrapped, then continue.) Place the potatoes directly into the low coals of the fire. Alternatively, you can put the potato onto a grill grate if preferred. There will be less chance of it burning on a grate but it may take longer to cook.

With tongs, flip the potato over every few minutes to ensure even heating. After 20 minutes, remove the potato from the fire. Using oven mitts or other heat protection, give the potato a light squeeze. When it feels soft and compressible, it should be done cooking.

Serve with your choice of condiments; sour cream, cheddar cheese, bacon bits and butter are popular choices.

Another great way to roast potatoes is to cut them into 1 inch chunks and place the cut pieces in foil. Add spices and olive oil as desired and seal foil, cover with second piece of foil and seal. Place in fire for 20 minutes and check for doneness. You can also place them in a Dutch oven at 425° using 31 coals with 21 on top and 10 on bottom.

❖　❖　❖　❖

Roasted Vegetables

Equipment

Garlic Press
(or Knife and Cutting Board)
Foil
Oven Mitts (or Leather Gloves)

Ingredients

1-2 cloves garlic
1 c. onion
1 c. mushrooms
1 c. broccoli florets
2 tbsp. olive oil
1 tsp. salt and pepper (or to taste)

Steps

Peel and crush garlic cloves. On a flat surface, place a piece of foil down. Prepare a second square the same size. Place all ingredients into the center of the foil and sprinkle with spices, salt, and pepper. Pinch and roll the foil together to make a packet. Wrap the second piece of foil around the packet and seal. Double wrapping will help cook the food more evenly and keep it from burning as easily. Place packet over heat on the fire grate. Turn every few minutes to ensure even cooking. Cook for about 15 to 20 minutes.

Alternatively you can roast the vegetables by placing them in a Dutch oven at 425° using 31 coals with 21 on top and 10 on bottom for about 20 minutes.

❖   ❖   ❖   ❖

Stuffed Avocados

Equipment

Knife
Cutting Board
Mixing bowl
Spoon

Ingredients

1 c. mayonnaise
Juice of ½ lemon
½ c. celery (finely chopped)
¼ c. carrots (shredded)
1/3 c. tomato (chopped)
1 tsp. garlic salt
½ tsp. Chili powder
3 c. bay shrimp (pre-cooked)
4-5 avocados
1 tbsp. parsley

Steps

In a mixing bowl, blend together mayonnaise, lemon juice, celery, carrots, tomato, garlic salt, chili powder, and shrimp. Halve the avocados and discard pits. Spoon the mayonnaise mixture into the pit hole and on top of avocados. Sprinkle with chopped parsley and serve.

❖　❖　❖　❖

Mom's Mush-erole (Mushroom Casserole)

My mother used to make this for special occasions. I've included it in this book for campfire cooking because it is one of my favorite recipes of all time. It is a difficult task over a fire so I do it in my RV oven but you can also do this in a Dutch oven if you desire. Once you have made this once it will become your favorite as well. If you plan on doing this in a Dutch oven then I recommend starting at home because of the difficulty level and the fact that it needs to rest for the first 24 hours under refrigeration before cooking.

Equipment

Cutting Board
Knife
Dutch Oven
(with Lid)
Skillet
Spoon

Ingredients

1 lb. fresh mushrooms
1 clove crushed garlic
½ c. butter
½ c. chopped onions
½ c. chopped celery
½ c. mayonnaise

10 – 12 slices of bread
¼ c. butter
1 tsp. salt and pepper
2 eggs
1 ½ c. milk
1 can cream of mushroom soup
¼ lb cheddar cheese
bread crumbs

Steps

Sauté mushrooms and garlic in 1/2 cup butter for 5 minutes. Remove from heat and add onions, celery and mayonnaise. Salt and pepper to taste mix well and set aside. Grease a large Dutch oven or baking dish if you have an oven. Brush bread with melted butter and place half in baking dish, covering the bottom. Spread mushroom mixture over bread. Top with remaining bread so that the mixture is covered. Mix eggs and milk and pour evenly over casserole.

Cover with lid and place in refrigerator overnight the day before you leave for your cook out. When ready to bake, spread with mushroom soup and sprinkle with grated cheese and bread crumbs. Bake at around 300° using 21 coals with 15 on top and 6 on bottom for 1 hour or until top is brown. If using an oven, cover with foil and bake for 40 minutes, remove foil and bake for another 20.

❖　❖　❖　❖

Pasta Salad

Equipment

Mixing bowl
Spoon

Ingredients

1 package spiral pasta
1 c. olive oil or mayonnaise (or add amounts to taste)
1 tbsp. minced garlic
½ c. diced black olives
½ c. diced yellow peppers
½ c. diced red peppers
1 small jar sliced artichoke hearts, drained
1 tsp. salt
½ tsp. pepper
1 tsp. basil
1 tsp. oregano
1 tbsp. parsley

Steps

Prepare pasta by cooking it al dente. Drain water and cool pasta. In large mixing bowl mix pasta with all the other ingredients, mix well and cover bowl. Store the salad in a cooler with ice for about an hour before serving. Serve cold.

❖　❖　❖　❖

Scallop Potatoes

Equipment

Dutch Oven
Spoon

Ingredients

6 c. thinly sliced peeled potatoes
1-1/2 c. chopped fully cooked ham
6 tbsp. butter
1/4 c. all-purpose flour
1 tsp. dried parsley
1 tsp. dried basil
1 tsp. salt
1/2 tsp. dried thyme
1/4 tsp. pepper
3 c. milk or cream
1 small onion, grated
1 package sliced mushrooms
1 c. Swiss cheese (final 15 minutes of baking)
1/2 c. bread crumbs (final 15 minutes of baking)

Steps

In a large saucepan, melt 4 tablespoons butter. Stir in flour, parsley, basil, salt, thyme, onion and pepper until smooth. Gradually add milk and bring to a low simmer. Cook and stir for about 2 minutes. Combine potatoes, ham and mix with sauce in Dutch oven. Cover Dutch oven and bake at 375° using 27 coals with 18 on top and 9 on bottom for 65-75 minutes or until potatoes are almost tender. In the last 15 minutes of cooking sprinkle the top with bread crumbs and cheese if desired. Place lid back on and place most of the coals on top of the oven to brown checking frequently. If using an oven leave uncovered for the last 15 minutes for browning.

❖ ❖ ❖ ❖

Campfire Green Bean Casserole

Equipment

Dutch Oven
Mixing Bowl
Spoon

Ingredients

3 c. cooked French style green beans (or canned)
1 can (10oz) cream of mushroom soup
¼ c. diced onion
¾ c. milk
1 c. mushrooms
1 1/3 c. French fried onions

½ c. bacon bits (optional)
1 c. cheddar cheese
1 tsp. parsley
½ tsp. salt
½ tsp. pepper
1 tbsp. garlic bread crumbs

Steps

Sauté onion and mushrooms over medium heat for about 5 minutes. Place the mushroom soup, milk, salt and pepper in a medium sized Dutch oven. Stir in beans, sautéed mushrooms and onions, bacon bits, cheese and 2/3 cup of the French fried onions. Reserve the rest of the French fried onions for later. Bake at 350° with 25 coals using 17 on top and 8 on bottom for 30 minutes. Then top with the remaining 2/3 cup fried onions and bread crumbs and bake for 5 more minutes with most coals on top or until onions are lightly browned on top.

Home Fries

Equipment

Cast Iron Pan
Spatula
Lid or Tin Foil

Ingredients

5 or 6 medium to large Yukon
gold potatoes
3 tbsp. olive oil
1 tbsp. butter
(optional, added for flavor)
1 tsp. salt
1 tsp. pepper
1 tsp. crushed red pepper
1 tsp. garlic powder or minced
(optional)
1 tsp. parsley

Steps

Heat cast iron pan over medium low heat and add oil and butter. Cube potatoes into ½ to ¾ inch cubes and toss into the pan and cook stirring occasionally about every 5 minutes. Keep covered in between stirring. Cook for 15 minutes and add the rest of the ingredients. Cook another 5 to 10 minutes or until potatoes are soft and not mushy.

❖   ❖   ❖   ❖

Baked Sweet Potatoes

Equipment

Foil

Ingredients

2 medium sweet potatoes
1 tsp. olive oil
1 tsp. garlic salt

Steps

Wash potatoes and let dry or dry with a paper towel. Cut a piece of foil large enough to cover the size of your potato. Place the potato on the foil and rub the olive oil all over the potato making sure to cover all parts. Sprinkle garlic salt all over, wrap the potato in foil and place in fire or over the fire for 15 minutes or until potato is just soft. Serve with butter.

❖   ❖   ❖   ❖

Don's Flaming Onion

This recipe was given to me by a guy I only camped with once. It is a really good side dish or snack if you love onions.

Equipment

Knife
Cutting Board
Basting Brush

Ingredients

4 Walla Walla sweet onions
2 tbsp. olive oil
salt and pepper (to taste)

Steps

Cut the tops off of an onion and peel off the outer layers. Starting at the center top, slice downward through the onion to within ½ to 1 inch intervals leaving about an inch at the bottom intact. The onion should spread out into a sort of flower shape if done correctly. Baste the onion with olive oil and spice with salt and pepper. If you like, add garlic powder or other spices. Repeat for all onions. Wrap in foil and place on fire or bake in Dutch oven at around 400° for about 20 to 30 minutes or until done.

The flaming onion about halfway cooked. If the onion appears uncooked re-wrap and continue cooking.

5
Poultry

Poultry is easy to prepare and a camping favorite. It can be grilled, spit-roasted, baked, or pan fried, and works beautifully in casseroles and many other types of recipes. It is also very forgiving, and is a great choice for both the beginner and the experienced campfire cook. The most important thing is to make sure the chicken is cooked thoroughly.

It should be said that I always cook chicken on the first day or two of any camping trip. The reason why is that raw chicken can quickly go bad in a cooler. This is a safety preference that I recommend and no one has ever gotten sick from eating my chicken. So when I plan chicken into my menu for a camping trip I always cook it as soon as possible.

The Original River Chicken Recipe

This recipe is very simple, but it makes for some delicious chicken. It can also be doubled extremely easily by simply preparing and roasting two chickens together on the spit.

Equipment

Cooking Spit
(or battery operated Rotisserie)
Foil
Plates
Cutting Board

Ingredients

1 whole roasting chicken
1 small bag of flavored chips
(or other rub of your choice)

Steps

Prepare the spit:

If a fire isn't already burning, set up a large fire. Light the fire, and let it burn down for at least an hour until you have some nice hot coals. You can use the intervening time to prepare the recipe. When the fire has been burning for a while, place the spit supports an appropriate distance apart on either side of the coals. If you are using a rotisserie, follow the directions for setting it up and be sure to use the rotisserie manufacturer's guidelines to avoid injury.

Prepare the rub:

The second step is to prepare the rub. If you are making the true Original River Chicken Recipe, you will need to crush the chips. To do this, place the chips in a zip lock bag and squeeze out the air in the bag. Use something hard to pulverize the chips inside the bag until they are finely crushed. Canned food works well if you roll it over the bag, but you can use a rock or pretty much anything hard so long as you're careful to avoid tearing the bag. Once the chips have been crushed to your satisfaction, set the bag aside.

Prepare the chicken:

First remove the giblets from inside the cavity of the chicken and dispose of them or save them for a broth or gravy later. Slide the chicken onto the spit rod, inserting the rod into the cavity of the chicken. Push carefully until the rod passes completely through the other end of the chicken. The spit rod may be very sharp; be careful to avoid poking your hand. Secure the chicken with spit forks if possible. Then open the bag of crushed chips or grab your own rub and rub the contents over the entire surface of the chicken. If you have some cooking twine, secure the legs to each other and bend the wings behind each other or tie them down. Be sure you wash your hands thoroughly with soap and warm water after handling raw meat. I often use surgeon's gloves to keep my hands from contaminating anything else while I'm preparing the chicken.

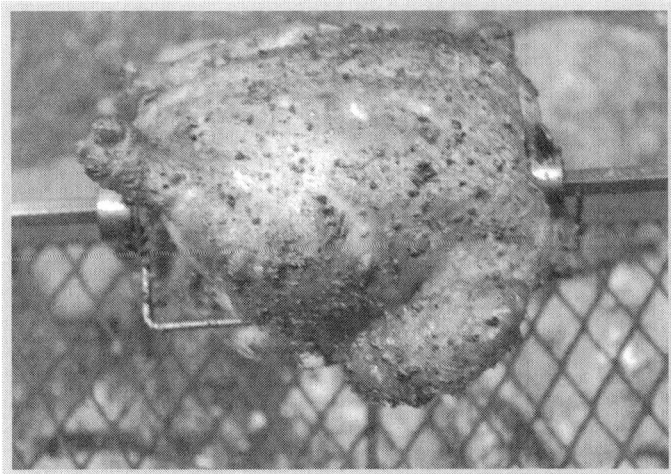

It is a lot of fun to watch a chicken cook on a spit.

Cook the chicken:

Place the spit rod onto its supports, suspending the chicken over the fire. The flames should rise to just below the chicken and barely kiss its skin. It will take approximately 2 hours for the chicken to roast. You will need to manually turn the spit a quarter turn every 10 minutes or so (if you do not have a motorized spit) so that all sides cook properly. Watch the chicken. The skin should start to brown slightly after about several minutes. After about an hour of cooking juice should begin dripping from the chicken. At this point you may wish to turn the spit more often to keep the juices flowing around, rather than out of, the chicken. Turning the chicken also helps to baste it. If the chicken seems to be cooking too quickly then splash a little water on the fire to slow down the burn and thus the cooking. If it seems to be cooking too slowly you can add a bit more wood to the fire. After a couple hours, the chicken should be a dark golden-brown color. I suggest using a meat thermometer if you wish to be sure the chicken is thoroughly cooked, or you can just see if the legs and wings come easily off of the body. If they do the chicken is probably ready to eat. I like to be on the safe side and use a thermometer.

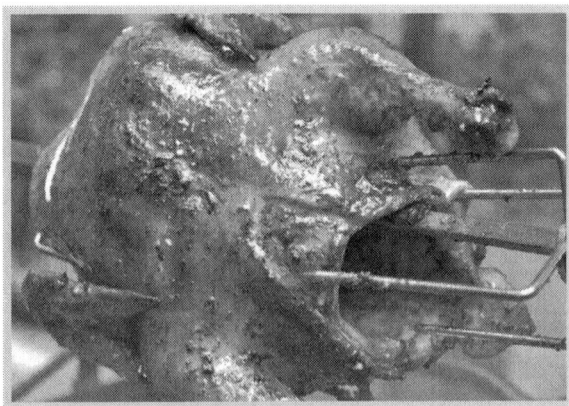

Sometimes the forks can become loose. You can use leather gloves to re-tighten the forks and keep the chicken in place.

Remove the spit rod from its supports. It will be very hot so use gloves. Slide the chicken off the rod onto a cutting board and set the spit rod back on its supports or someplace safe to cool. You may wish to have assistance for this step. Let the chicken stand covered in foil for about 20 minutes to rest. Lastly, carve, serve, and enjoy!

❖   ❖   ❖   ❖

Left Over River Chicken Sandwich's (Best Grilled Cheese Ever)

Equipment

Pie Iron

Ingredients

2 pieces of bread
1 to 2 pieces of cheese
¼ to ½ cup left over chicken chopped
Butter

Steps

Heat the pie iron in the fire for about 1 to 2 minutes. Remove from heat and carefully (making sure not to touch the iron) separate the irons and melt butter in both sides. Place an iron on a flat surface and place bread on top of one of the irons, then top the bread with cheese, then chicken and finally the second piece of bread. Carefully place the irons together sealing in the sandwich. Place over coals for at least 3 minutes on each side. Check often, when the bread is light brown the sandwich is done. Caution, the insides will be very hot.

The perfect sandwich

Darcie's River Chicken Pot Pie

My good friend Darcie was there the first day I ate a river chicken. Since that day and all the fodder that has ensued, she has come up with her own river chicken recipe. This book would not be complete without a recipe from one of the River Chicken originators.

Equipment

Dutch Oven
(with lid)
Saucepan
Cooking Spoon
Knife
Cutting Board
Skillet

Ingredients

2 pre-made pie crusts (store bought or homemade)
10 oz. mixed peas and carrots
½ onion (minced)
½ c. sliced mushrooms
½ stick butter
½ tsp. salt
½ tsp. sage

1/8 tsp. ground black pepper
2 c. water
¾ c. milk
1 tbsp. chicken bouillon
3 c. pre-cooked cubed chicken
¼ c. parsley

(Be sure to pick out any ashes, rocks, and sticks from the weekend camping trip; Doritos are OK)

Steps for Filling

Cook peas and carrots in a couple tbsp. water over low-medium heat until just slightly softened and set aside. Chop and sauté onion and mushrooms in butter over low-medium heat until onions are translucent. Raise heat to medium. Stir in flour, salt, sage, and pepper. Add chicken bouillon, milk, and remaining water. Cook and stir until thickened and bubbly. Cook and stir 1 to 2 minutes more, then mix in vegetables, chicken and parsley, stir until bubbly again.

Pour mixture into dough-lined Dutch oven (an oven liner or aluminum pie pan comes in handy here) and top with reserved dough. Pinch dough together and cut slits in the top. Cover Dutch oven and place 14 coals on top and 7 on bottom to achieve 350° and cook or until crust is golden brown.

Chicken Soup with Dumplings

Equipment

Large Dutch
Oven; with Lid
2 C. Measure
(or Mixing Bowl)
Knife
Cutting Board
Small Saucepan
Wire Whisk

Ingredients

3 quarts chicken broth
(or use less broth and add
water)
2 c. carrots
3 c. mushrooms
2 c. celery
2 cloves garlic
4 tbsp. butter
4 tbsp. flour
3 c. boneless chicken
1 tbsp. salt (to taste)

1 tsp. pepper
(to taste)
1 tsp. basil
(optional)
1 tsp. oregano
(optional)
1 tsp. thyme
(optional)
2 c. potatoes cubed
(optional)
1 can pre-made
biscuits

Steps

Bring broth to a slow simmer over low-medium heat, reserving 1 C. at room temperature. While broth is heating, chop carrots, mushrooms, and celery; set aside. Peel and mince garlic and set aside. Wash and cube potatoes if using. In a small saucepan, melt butter over low heat. When butter is fully melted, whisk in flour a little bit at a time. Cook flour-butter mixture for 3 or 4 minutes until is well blended, add reserved broth and whisk rapidly until blended. This roux will thicken up the soup for a hearty stock. Add the roux to the broth and add potatoes and bring back to a simmer and cook for 10 to 15 minutes. Now add the vegetables and stir in all remaining ingredients. Bring back up to a slow simmer, stirring every 15 minutes or so and let simmer for about 30 minutes more while you prepare the dumplings (test the potatoes for doneness before add dumplings).

Cut each of the biscuits into halves or quarters and place them into simmering broth. Cook for 10 to 15 minutes in the broth, or until done. If you choose to make your own dumplings from scratch this is the time to add them.

Ladle into bowls, garnish with parsley, and serve.

❖   ❖   ❖   ❖

Chicken 'n Rice

Equipment

Dutch Oven (with Lid)

Ingredients

water or broth
2-6 pieces boneless chicken
1 box chicken flavored rice package
¼ onion
1 c. spinach
1 c. mushrooms

Steps

Chop onion and mushrooms. Follow the directions on the Rice-a-Roni box to cook the rice in the Dutch oven, but add about ½ C. less water than recommended on the box then add all the vegetables and stir. Add whole boned chicken parts, I usually use thighs and place them on top of the rice. Cover and place coals under and on top of Dutch oven at 375°. This is about 27 coals, 18 on top and 9 on bottom. Check the chicken and rice for doneness after 30 45 minutes, and then every 5 to 10 minutes until chicken and rice is fully cooked.

❖   ❖   ❖   ❖

Shanna Montana's Mountain Hobo Stew

Equipment

Knife
Cutting Board
Aluminum Foil

Ingredients

1 small potato (per serving)
½ small onion (per serving)
½ small carrot (per serving)
¼ small zucchini (per serving)
¼ small yellow squash (per serving)
½ small turnip
(or rutabaga; or both for kicks)
½ small beet (per serving)
1 clove garlic (per serving)
4 oz. turkey kielbasa (per serving)
1 tbsp. butter (or olive oil; to taste)

Steps

Dice potato and onion. Slice carrot, zucchini, squash, turnip, rutabaga, beet, and any other veggies desired; slice kielbasa into coins. Peel and mince garlic. Lay aluminum foil onto a flat surface, shiny side up. Place a small amount of each of the mixed ingredients into center of foil, add butter (or olive oil), and fold foil up around ingredients to create a packet. Pinch shut and wrap entire packet in a second piece of foil, pinching that shut as well. Place foil packet directly into a low fire or on the coals. Cook for 20 minutes or until desired doneness is achieved.

*This recipe and Shanna Montana's Fantastic Mountain Trout courtesy of my wonderful friend Shanna.

❖   ❖   ❖   ❖

Beer Butt (or Beer Can) Chicken

This is one of my favorite ways to cook a chicken. The end result is one of the juiciest chickens you will ever sink your teeth into. I'm told you can use water and get the same results which saves the beer for drinking.

Equipment

Paper Towel
Beer Butt Chicken Roaster
Can opener
Twine
Aluminum Foil
(You can substitute a large lid from a barbeque grill or roasting pan or any such similar item that is tall enough to mostly cover the roasting chicken.)
High Heat Baking Dish
(large enough to hold the entire chicken)
Water
(for controlling flare ups from the fire)

Ingredients

1 roasting chicken
¼ cup rub or seasonings
1 can of beer
olive oil
1 gallon brine (optional)

Steps

Prepare the fire: You will want a low fire for this dish, with many coals and not much flame, so start it at least one hour prior to cooking and let it burn down. Also, if you plan to soak the chicken in brine do so at least 8 hours prior to cooking.

Prepare the roaster:

Set the beer can chicken roaster into the baking dish or on the fire grate. Use a can opener to open the entire top of a can of beer. I usually pour about a quarter of the beer out or into a glass (I admit I like to drink it), then place the can with the remaining beer into the roaster beer can roaster. Alternatively you can use the entire can.

Prepare the chicken:

Start by removing the giblets from the cavity of the chicken and discard them or you can save them for use later. Brine the chicken the day before the camping trip. I sometimes brine the chicken in a freezer bag and transport it in the brine, removing it when I am ready to cook.

When you are ready to roast, slide the chicken down over the beer roaster, so that the beer can is inside the cavity of the chicken. Tie the chicken legs together with twine and tuck the wingtips underneath the larger part of the wings so that they do not burn when roasting. If you don't have string then wrap the legs and wings individually in foil to prevent burning. Pat the chicken dry with the paper towel. Next, rub the chicken with a little olive oil, and then coat the chicken liberally with seasoning rub.

Place foil or a large cover over the chicken to retain the heat. If the chicken is in a baking dish, press two or three pieces of foil together at their edges to make one wider piece. Drape this over the chicken and compress the foil around the edges of the baking dish, creating a loose dome. This will hold in heat and moisture as the chicken roasts. If you are using a grill lid or any other type of cover, place it over the chicken once you have set the chicken on the fire grate.

Set the roaster carefully over of the fire, making sure the chicken does not tip over. The flames should be no higher than the bottom of the chicken; if the flames are too high, sprinkle a bit of water onto the fire to cool it slightly. Juices should begin dripping from the chicken into the baking dish or on the fire shortly after you place the dish on the heat.

Cook for at least an hour and a half, remove the cover and check the internal temperature of the chicken. If the fire is not providing enough heat, add a small amount of wood to the coals and continue to roast the chicken. Check the chicken every 10-15 minutes from this point on till it reaches the correct internal temperature. Cooking time will vary depending on the size of the chicken and the heat of the fire. When you feel that the chicken is adequately cooked, check to see whether the legs pull easily off the body (an indicator of doneness) or test with a meat thermometer in the thickest part of the thigh to ensure that the internal temperature of the chicken has reached 165°-170°. When the chicken is done, remove the baking dish from the fire. I often cook to 175° just to be safe and usually don't have issues with dryness. The beer helps to keep the bird moist. Lift the chicken off of the beer butt roaster. Be careful, as the beer can and liquid inside will still be very hot. Place the chicken onto a plate or cutting board, cover loosely with foil and let the chicken rest for 15-20 minutes. Carve and serve the tender, juicy meat with your favorite side.

❖   ❖   ❖   ❖

Fried Chicken

Fried chicken is one of the ultimate comfort foods and one of my all-time favorites, so it must be included in this book.

Regardless of which cooking method you choose, you will want to use a good cast iron pan with a lid. Also, soak the chicken either in buttermilk or a salty poultry brine for at least 4 hours. If you are using buttermilk then it can soak for up to 24 hours. If soaking the chicken in salt brine then don't overdo it; eight hours should be the maximum soaking time.

Deep Fry Method

Deep frying chicken can be done over a campfire, but I have found that it can be difficult to maintain a good steady hot temperature so I prefer to use a stove and a good meat thermometer to ensure that the chicken is thoroughly cooked. Using a camp stove makes it a much easier process but can be messy so have lots of paper towels available. The consistent heat of a camp stove will help to make sure the chicken is fully cooked and crispy. Again I like to have a thermometer around to make sure the chicken is at least 160°.

Equipment

Tongs
(or Slotted Spoon)
Dutch oven
(or deep Frying Pan)
Meat Thermometer
Large Mixing Bowl
Small Mixing Bowl
Wire Whisk
2 Wire Racks
Camp Stove

Ingredients

4 to 6 chicken pieces
(use the cuts of your choice)
1 qt. buttermilk
2 c. flour
2 tbsp. paprika
2 tsp. Chili powder
1 tsp. cayenne pepper
2 tbsp. salt
(or salt to taste)

1 tsp. pepper
2 food storage bags
butter (optional)
2 eggs
peanut oil
(or canola oil)
2 food storage bags
butter (optional)
2 eggs
peanut oil
(or canola oil)

Steps

There are three parts to the preparation of fried chicken – a dry coating, an egg wash, and a final coating. The first coating helps to provide a surface to which the egg wash will bind and adds flavor to the meat. The egg wash and the second coating provide the delicious crispy exterior that is the hallmark of fried chicken.

Begin heating the oil, a Dutch oven is a good choice for this; a deep frying pan may work if a Dutch oven is not an option. The oil should reach at approximately 350° for proper cooking. Use a stove to achieve these temperatures.

Next, mix all the dry ingredients together in the mixing bowl. Separate half of the mixture into a food storage bag and the other half into a wide bowl or plate. Set the plate aside. One by one, place each piece of chicken into the bag and shake until the chicken is well coated in the flour/spice mixture, then remove it from the bag and set it aside to rest a few minutes.

Once all the chicken pieces are coated, whisk the eggs together thoroughly in the small mixing bowl to make the egg wash. Now lay out the components in the following order (this will make this process go more smoothly). Start with the chicken pieces, then the egg wash, the remaining plate of flour mixture, and a wire rack or plate. Now take a piece of chicken and dip it in the egg wash, then place it onto the plate of flour/spice mixture and gently manipulate until the chicken is thoroughly coated in flour. Remove the chicken piece from the plate and set it onto the wire rack. Do this with all remaining pieces of chicken. Let the pieces rest for at about 10 minutes on the rack. This will give the coating time to 'set' so it will fry up properly without disintegrating.

While the chicken is resting, make sure the cooking oil has reached the proper frying temperature of approximately 325° to 350°. After the chicken has rested for at least 10 minutes, use the tongs or slotted spoon to very carefully submerge the chicken pieces into the hot oil, making sure that no pieces overlap or touch; they will not cook correctly if the pan is overcrowded. You may need to fry more than one batch of chicken if you cannot fit all pieces.

Fry the chicken for about 15 to 20 minutes, making sure that the oil temperature is maintained at around 350°. While the chicken is frying, place the second rack or a plate next to the Dutch oven with a paper towel to catch any oil drip. When the chicken is done pull out the chicken with tongs and place on the rack or plate. Remove all the chicken from the hot oil and carefully place it on the rack to drain for 3-5 minutes.

If you need to add more oil in order to fry pieces that did not fit in the first batch, make sure the oil is heated to the proper temperature before you begin.

Pan Fry Method

Pan frying is the way my mother fried chicken back in the day. When I went off to college, I thought I'd try to make some myself, but when I tossed a chicken thigh into a small skillet with just a little butter, no spices and no coating, needless to say it didn't turn out very well. Many years passed before I tried it again. This time with much better results.

With time on my hands due to being laid off, I decided to experiment with some dishes I had never made well. A little comfort food seemed in order after a job loss, so I went to work with fried chicken. Thanks to the advent of the Internet I watched a video that showed me how to make good fried chicken and this time it not only came out edible but quite good. I tweaked the recipe over the next few years to try to make it "just like mom used to make." The pan-fried chicken recipe in *The Culinary Camper* is as close as I've been able to come to the flavor that I loved so much as a kid. It is best made with butter, but you can use Canola oil if you prefer. And I also prefer to use a camp stove with this recipe since it's much easier to keep the heat consistent.

Equipment

Deep Frying Pan
Slotted Spatula
Camp Stove

Ingredients

4 to 6 chicken pieces (use the cuts of your choice)
2 c. flour
2 tbsp. paprika
1 tsp. Chili powder (add more for more zing)
1 tsp. cayenne pepper
2 tbsp. salt (or salt to taste)
1 tsp. pepper
½ c. butter (optional for flavor)
½ to 1 c. canola oil

Steps

This type of chicken is a quite a bit easier than the deep fry method so I have to admit I use this recipe more often. Mix all the dry ingredients in a bag. Place the chicken in the bag and toss to coat well. Set chicken aside. Add the oil to the frying pan at a medium heat and add butter to melt if using. Cook over medium heat for 10-15 minutes on each side, until juices run clear and chicken is opaque and white throughout.

My mother always served this with rice and a vegetable; I love it with steamed white rice with lots of butter. This is not something I eat often but still love it to this day.

❖   ❖   ❖   ❖

Grilled Chicken

Equipment

Grill
Tongs or Spatula
Sharp Knife
Meat Thermometer (optional)
Water (optional)

Ingredients

6 pieces of chicken
1 tsp. salt and pepper
1 tsp. garlic powder
(Alternatively, use your favorite rub liberally)

Steps

Start the fire at least one hour prior to cooking and let it burn down. Set the grill rack over the coals. Apply the spices to each piece of chicken. Place the pieces onto the grill. When the chicken pieces begin to turn white around the top edges, flip each piece of chicken over using tongs or a spatula. This will probably take at least 20 minutes or more, but smaller pieces will cook faster than larger ones. If the chicken pieces appear to have begun to burn on the bottom, sprinkle a bit of water onto the coals or spread them out a bit to reduce the heat of the fire. Cook another 20 minutes.

Test for doneness by inserting a meat thermometer into the center of the thickest piece of chicken. If it reaches 165°, the chicken is done. Alternately, insert a sharp knife into the thickest piece. The chicken is probably fully cooked if the meat juices run clear. Remove chicken pieces from the grill with tongs and serve.

❖   ❖   ❖   ❖

Grilled Stuffed Chicken

Equipment

Heavy Duty Plastic Wrap
Meat Hammer
Cutting Board
Knife
2 Frying pans
Spoon
Skewers (or Wooden Picks)
Fork

Ingredients

2 to 4 broiler/fryer chicken breasts (boneless)
1 packages Canadian bacon
1 packages sliced Swiss cheese
½ c. mushrooms sliced
1 tbsp. olive oil
1 tsp. salt and pepper (to taste)
1 tsp. garlic powder

Steps

Create a cavity in each breast by sliding the knife into the side of the breast and sweeping the blade back and forth within the meat until a slit is cut on the side. Stuff chicken with one piece of Canadian bacon and one piece of cheese and a few mushrooms. Pierce the chicken with a skewer on the open side to seal in the ingredients.

Brush chicken with olive oil and sprinkle with salt, pepper and garlic powder. Grill for about 10 minutes or until brown, then carefully flip and grill for another 10 minutes. Chicken is done when it can easily be pierced with a fork and juices run clear.

I used kabob skewers to seal these large filets.

❖   ❖   ❖   ❖

Chicken Cordon Bleu

Don't let the name of this recipe fool you, this is a pretty simple recipe that tastes great.

Equipment

Cutting Board
Frying Pan (or Grill)
Knife
Basting Brush

Ingredients

2 to 4 boneless skinless chicken breast halves
4 oz. ham (shaved)
4 - 1 oz. slices of Swiss cheese
4 tbsp. dijon mustard
salt and pepper (to taste)

Steps

Create a cavity in each breast by sliding the knife into the top of the breast and sweeping the blade back and forth within the meat.

Wrap ham around each slice of cheese and carefully insert into the cavity in each breast. Baste the breasts with Dijon mustard then sprinkle lightly with salt and pepper. Pan fry in olive oil or grill for about 10 minutes on each side.

❖   ❖   ❖   ❖

Chicken Piccata

This sauce can be tricky to do outside but it is really tasty.

Equipment

Frying Pan
Spatula
2 Saucepans (or Dutch Ovens)
Wire Wisk
Colander
Ladle (or Cooking Spoon)

Ingredients

1 chicken breasts slice in small strips
2 tbsp. olive oil
piccata sauce (see Chapter 3)
1 package linguini noodles
1 tsp. salt (optional)
1 tbsp. parmesan cheese

Steps

Cut chicken into bite sized strips and brown in olive oil.

After browning for about 5 to 10 minutes, set aside. Prepare the Piccata Sauce from chapter 3. When the sauce is simmering, add the chicken. Begin boiling water for the noodles, adding salt if desired.

Cook the noodles al dente, strain and plate. Ladle the desired amount of sauce onto the noodles and sprinkle with parmesan cheese.

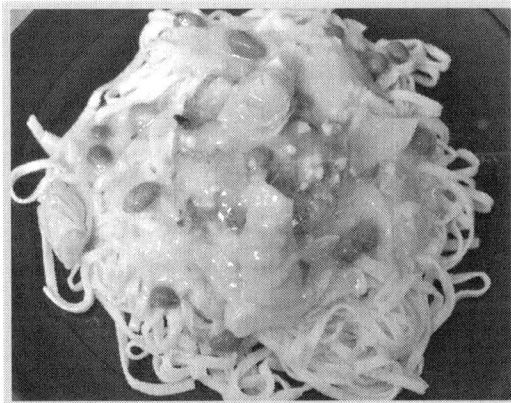

❖   ❖   ❖   ❖

Garlic Chicken

Equipment

Deep frying pan
Knife
Cutting Board
Cooking Spoon

Ingredients

1 lb. boneless skinless chicken breast
½ c. chicken stock
2 tbsp. soy sauce
1 tbsp. cornstarch
1 tbsp. dry white wine
1 tbsp. olive oil
½ 8 oz. can water chestnuts
(drained and sliced)
10 cloves garlic (chopped)
6 oz. fresh mushrooms (sliced)
4 green onions (thinly sliced)
1 tsp. salt
½ tsp. pepper

Steps

Brown chicken breast and remove from heat. Cut chicken into half-inch strips and set aside. Mix stock, soy sauce, cornstarch, wine, oil and water chestnuts into same pan. Stir slowly for about 5 minutes on medium heat. Add garlic, mushrooms, green onions, chicken, salt, and pepper. Cook another 5 minutes, stirring occasionally.

Serve over rice or noodles.

❖   ❖   ❖   ❖

Chicken Florentine

Equipment

Large Cast Iron
Skillet
Spatula
Large Bowl
Wire Whisk
(or Cooking Spoon)

Ingredients

1 lb. boneless skin-less chicken breast or thigh (cubed)
2 tbsp. butter (or margarine)
2 c. mushrooms (sliced)
½ c. chopped onion
½ c. green onion (chopped)
1 c. spinach (chopped)
3 tbsp. flour

1 c. chicken broth
1 c. evaporated milk
2 tbsp. parmesan cheese (grated)
½ c. black olives (sliced)
1½ tsp. garlic
1 tsp. salt
½ tsp. pepper
½ tsp. red pepper
½ tsp. dried parsley
½ tsp. dried basil
½ tsp. dried oregano

Steps

Over medium-high heat, cook cubed chicken in the large skillet until juices run clear. Transfer the chicken from the skillet into a bowl and set it aside. Melt 1 tbsp. butter in the skillet. Add mushrooms and onions and stir constantly for 2 minutes. Add spinach, continuing to stir until the spinach is wilted. Add the cooked spinach mixture to the bowl holding the chicken and again set aside. Stir the flour and the remaining butter together in the skillet until well blended, then whisk in broth. Add evaporated milk and stir until thickened. Once the sauce has thickened, combine all ingredients, including those you had previously set aside, in the skillet and simmer for 5 minutes. Serve with rice or pasta.

Alternate recipe:

Roll out each biscuit in from a tin of pre made biscuits and place in a cup or muffin tin for support so that they form a small bowl. Scoop some of the mixture into the cup and seal the biscuit around the mixture. Place each in a Dutch oven with a lid. Cook at 350° or 25 coals. Use 17 on top / 8 on bottom and cook for 15 minutes or until browned.

❖   ❖   ❖   ❖

Turkey Burgers

Equipment

Mixing Bowl
Skillet (or Grill)
Spatula

Ingredients

1 p. ground turkey
1 tbsp. olive oil
1 tsp. kosher salt
½ tsp. black pepper
1/3 tsp. paprika
1 tsp. oregano
1 tbsp. Worcestershire sauce
½ c. pepper jack cheese
(shredded)
¼ c. jalapeño pepper

Steps

Mix all ingredients thoroughly; form mixture into patties about ½ inch thick and about 3 inches in diameter. Cook in frying pan for about 5 minutes each side. Serve on a bun with your favorite condiments.

❖   ❖   ❖   ❖

Deno Beano's Fireside Chili

Equipment

Dutch Oven (with Lid)

Ingredients

1 package ground chicken sausage
1 can black beans
2 cans kidney beans
1 poblano pepper diced
1 green chili diced
1 tomato diced
1 tsp. ghost salt
1 ½ tbsp. chili powder
1 tsp. oregano
1 tsp. basil
1 tsp. salt and pepper
1 tbsp. garlic
1 tbsp. olive oil

Steps

Warm olive oil, brown sausage in oil and stir in garlic. Add cans of beans with liquid - do not drain. Add rest of ingredients and stir. Allow to simmer for 90 minutes.

❖   ❖   ❖   ❖

6
Beef

Ground Beef Recipes

When it comes to hamburgers I consider myself a bit of a snob. I love burgers; I've worked in several fast food places and learned how to cook some very delicious burgers. Here are a few key points I've found effective when making burgers.

If you are making your own patties, mix some dry spices into the meat to add flavor. Do not use wet spices or sauces unless it's just a tbsp. or so because your burgers could end up a big sloppy mess. I had a friend pour about a half of a bottle of barbeque sauce into a pound of hamburger and it not only didn't cook well but it fell apart over the grill. That dinner turned into a vegetarian affair.

Cooked in a cast iron pan with double cheese. Yum!

For variety there are several different kinds of meat you can substitute, or add to ground beef. My personal favorite is buffalo, which is a healthy option because of its abundance of Omega 3 fatty acids and low overall fat content. Other options include ground chicken or turkey, elk, and veggie patties. (If using turkey for your burger be sure to add some spices and add a bit of olive oil since turkey tends to be dry.) For an extremely tasty (if unhealthy) twist on your burgers you can try topping with Canadian bacon, ham, pastrami, bleu cheese, a fried egg, sausages, sautéed mushrooms, or fried onion rings.

Hamburger is a lot like steak and how long you cook it depends on thickness and personal preference on rareness. The USDA recommends not eating rare or medium-rare ground meats because of potential contamination from bacteria due to processing methods; however, it is a personal choice for many people.

A cold bun on a burger is just wrong. Always, always, always toast your bun, brushed with olive oil or butter. This will improve your burger tenfold. In some restaurants buns are steamed, which is also good. The key is to have a hot bun to make a really delicious burger.

I always let people dress his or her own bun. Have a good assortment of condiments on hand to suit many tastes. At a minimum I like to have mayonnaise, ketchup, mustard, tartar sauce, and barbeque sauce. To supplement the condiments you may want some crispy bacon, fresh lettuce, avocado, sliced tomato, and dill pickles, or anything else you can think of that sounds tasty. Be creative!

Cheese-Stuffed Burgers

Equipment

Mixing Bowl
Cast Iron Skillet (or Grill)
Metal Spatula

Ingredients

1 lb. ground beef
¼ c. garlic bread crumbs
4 oz. cheese (try Boursin, cheddar or Colby jack; grated)
1 dash salt and pepper (to taste)

Steps

Mix the ground meat with the bread crumbs and a pinch or two of salt and pepper. Roll the meat into 4 equal balls. Poke a hole in the middle of each ball and place about an ounce worth of cheese in the hole. Press the ball down into a patty without squeezing out the cheese. Sprinkle with a little seasoning of salt and pepper on each side and grill over a fire. Serve with your favorite condiments and side.

❖　　❖　　❖　　❖

Beef Cups

Equipment

Cast Iron Skillet
Spatula
Cooking Spoon
Knife
Cutting Board
Measuring Cup (optional)
Dutch Oven (with lid)

Ingredients

shortening
(or other cooking grease)
3/4 lb. lean ground beef
2 cloves garlic
½ c. beef gravy
(canned or homemade)
1 tbsp. dried or fresh minced onion
1 pkg. refrigerated biscuit dough
(or dough of your choice)
½ c. shredded cheddar cheese

Steps

In a large heavy skillet over medium heat, cook beef until evenly browned. Drain excess fat. Peel and mince garlic. Add gravy, garlic, and onion to the beef. Simmer for a few minutes over low heat. While the mixture is simmering, grease the Dutch oven, including the sides.

Flatten a biscuit on the cutting board, and then with your fingers, form it into a pouch. You may want to place the dough into a measuring cup, muffin pan or something to hold the cup shape; make sure the dough extends over the edges of the device used to hold it. Spoon a portion of the meat mixture into each dough cup and add some cheese on top, leaving enough room to pinch the dough together. Bring the edges of the dough together and pinch closed, sealing the meat/cheese mixture inside. Place the pouch into the Dutch oven. Repeat with the remaining biscuits, making sure to set the dough cups as far apart as possible when you place them into the Dutch oven, do not over crowd.

Seal the Dutch oven and cook at around 350° using about 25 coals with 17 on top and 8 on bottom for 12 to 15 minutes until golden brown.

Use a knife to separate the dough cups after cooking if necessary.

These make for a tasty treat for lunch or dinner.

❖   ❖   ❖   ❖

Cheesy Burger Pockets

Equipment

Knife
Large Cutting
Board
Mixing Bowl
Cooking Spoon
Skillet
Rolling Pin
Dutch Oven
Basting Brush

Ingredients

1 small onion
1 lb. lean ground beef
or buffalo
2 tbsp. dill pickle relish
2 tbsp. grated parme-
san cheese
1 tbsp. mayonnaise
1 tbsp. ketchup
1 tsp. minced garlic
1 dash salt and
pepper (to taste)
2 tbsp. olive oil
2 tbsp. flour
1 lb. frozen bread
dough (thawed)
8 slices cheddar
cheese (or your
favorite cheese)
1 tbsp. butter

Steps

Peel and mince onion. Combine the ground beef, relish, onion, Parmesan cheese, mayonnaise, ketchup, garlic, salt, and pepper in a bowl. Stir well and form into 4 patties. Cook the patties with olive oil in a skillet over medium heat for about 4 or 5 minutes on each side.

Sprinkle a large cutting board liberally with flour. Divide the bread dough into 4 even pieces. Roll each piece into a flattened circle at least twice the size as the cheese slice. Place one slice of cheese in the center of a piece of dough. Place one of the cooled cooked beef patties on the cheese slice, and top with a second slice of cheese (if desired) on top.

Fold the dough up and over the edges of the meat and cheese and pinch the dough together around the edges, sealing it completely.

Arrange in Dutch oven with the seam side facing downward. Brush the tops with the melted butter.

Spread the dough out enough to cover the whole burger.

Cover and move to a warm area for 20 minutes to allow the dough to rise, rising times may vary according to the temperature. After dough has risen, cook at about 375° using 27 coals with 18 on top and 9 on bottom for about 20 minutes, or until dough appears fully baked and golden brown.

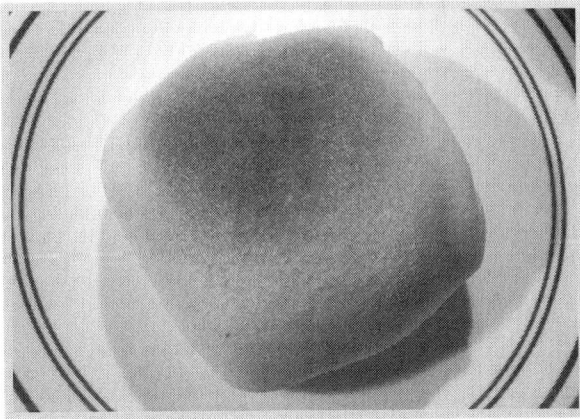

These were amazing.

❖   ❖   ❖   ❖

Beef Stew

Equipment

Soup Pot
(or Dutch Oven)
Slotted Cooking Spoon
Knife
Cutting Board
Large Skillet
Wire Whisk
Cooking Spoon
Vegetable Peeler

Ingredients

1 head garlic
4 q. beef stock
1-2 lb. stew beef
2 tbsp. Worcestershire sauce
2 tbsp. butter
½ c. flour (or cornstarch)
1 dash salt and pepper (to taste)
4 medium potatoes
2-4 carrots
2 stalks celery
1-2 large onions
1 - 12 oz can beer (optional)
1 pkg. pre-made biscuit dough
(or pre-made biscuits; optional)

Steps

Place the broth in the pot and put over medium heat. Peel and crush garlic and add to the broth. Add bay leaf to broth and cover. Cut stew meat into bite-sized chunks. In a large skillet over medium-high heat, brown stew meat with Worcestershire sauce. Transfer browned meat to broth. Save the reserving drippings from browning your meat and add butter and flour (or cornstarch) to drippings to make a roux; whisk until well blended. Stir the roux into the broth while it simmers. Simmer for one and a half to two hours.

Peel and quarter potatoes (if desired). Add salt, pepper and potatoes to broth; let simmer at a low heat for 20 minutes. Peel and chop celery, carrots and onion; add to broth. Let simmer another 10 to 20 minutes, or until the potatoes and vegetables are cooked. Remove pot from heat and let rest for about 10 minutes before serving.

Beef Pot Pie Alternative

As an alternative, you can turn this into a Beef Pot Pie by carefully placing biscuit dough (or pre-made biscuits) on top of the stew 10-20 minutes before the stew is finished cooking. Try to avoid wetting the biscuits as much as possible. Cover, and cook until biscuits are fully baked. Another option is to take puffed pastry and put it on top of the stew, cover in the Dutch oven and place 15 to 18 coals on top and bake for 20 minutes or until dough is cooked.

❖　❖　❖　❖

Corned Beef and Cabbage

Equipment

Dutch oven (with Lid)
Slotted Cooking Spoon

Ingredients

1 corned beef brisket
4 qt. water (or enough to cover the brisket)
3 carrots chopped into ½ inch bites
2 potatoes, cubed (optional)
½ green cabbage, chopped

Corned beef in the coals of the fire. Cover with lid and simmer slowly.

Steps

The key to cooking corned beef is to cook it at low heat for several hours. You must try to maintain a slow rolling simmer in a Dutch oven to cook the meat fully. Place brisket into Dutch oven and add enough water to completely cover the meat. Add the seasoning packet from the brisket. Cover, and place the Dutch oven either over the fire or into a bed of low coals. Add just enough coals to bring water to a slow rolling boil with a few on top as well. Maintain this level of heat for a minimum of 2 hours; 4-6 hours is preferable if your heat is low enough. 20-30 minutes before you want to serve your meal, add hard vegetables such as potatoes and carrots. Wait until the last 5 minutes to add cabbage.

❖   ❖   ❖   ❖

Cowboy Casserole

Equipment

Can Opener
Dutch Oven
(with Lid)

Ingredients

1½ lb. lean ground beef
1 can cream of mush-
room soup
1 can cheddar cheese
soup
½ c. milk
2 c. frozen or canned peas
(or spinach, corn, or green
beans)
2 c. tater tots
(or enough to top the
casserole)

1-2 c. cheddar
cheese
2 tbsp. parmesan
cheese
2 tsp. salt
1 tsp. pepper
1 tsp. basil
1 tsp. oregano
¼ tsp. cayenne
pepper or 4
shakes of ghost
salt

Steps

Brown the hamburger with salt and pepper and add browned meat to the Dutch oven. Add milk both cans of soup and the vegetable, spices, cheese and mix. Now top with a single layer of tater tots. Sprinkle lightly with parmesan cheese. Cover Dutch oven and cook at 375° with 27 coals with 18 on top and 9 on bottom for about 25 minutes or until tater tots are cooked.

❖   ❖   ❖   ❖

Hobo Stew (Tin Foil Dinners)

This is one of my favorite camp meals and is a great one to prepare at home and have for your first night's meal if you aren't going to have much time to prepare dinner. Having it ready to go makes it simple to get camp set up, get a campfire going, and then kick back with a beverage and relax while your dinner cooks.

Equipment

Heavy-Duty Aluminum Foil
Vegetable Peeler
Cutting Board
Knife

Ingredients

1 small potato
½ small onion
½ small carrot
½ c. sliced mushrooms
1 clove garlic
6 oz. hamburger
1 tsp. salt
½ tsp. pepper
1 or 2 pre-made biscuit dough
2 tbsp. barbeque sauce (optional)

Steps

Putting hobo stew together is simple. Lay out a large piece of aluminum foil. Peel carrot and potato. Chop potato into ½ to 1 inch cubed pieces and place in the center of the foil. Slice carrot into coins and place on top of the potatoes. Slice onion finely and place on top of carrots. Add mushrooms. Peel and mince garlic and add to foil. Add chunks of hamburger to the pile. By adding the hamburger on top, the juices from the meat will trickle down through the vegetables, flavoring and cooking them beautifully. Sprinkle with salt, pepper and whatever other spices you prefer. Top the pile with biscuit dough (or biscuit). Bring the foil up to make a packet enclosing the ingredients; pinch it tightly shut. Wrap packet in a second piece of foil and pinch that shut as well. Place packet in medium coals or on grill for 15-20 minutes, turning it often so it doesn't burn. After 20 minutes, carefully unwrap one edge (be careful – escaping steam will be extremely hot) and check to see if potatoes and meat have fully cooked. If necessary, re-close foil and toss back on the heat; otherwise, dig in and enjoy! Serve with barbeque sauce if desired.

❖ ❖ ❖ ❖

Kathleen's Tater Hobo Stew

Equipment

Aluminum Foil
Cutting Board
(or precut at home)
Knife

Ingredients

½ to 1 cup tater tots
¼ c. diced onion
½ c. diced celery
¼ c. diced carrot
¼ c. zucchini
¼ c. yellow squash
1 clove garlic
½ to 1 cup ground beef (optional)
1 tbsp. butter
(if not using optional ground beef)

Steps

Since Kathleen is vegetarian I thought I would make the meat optional. When she made me this dish she included it in everyone else's but hers.

Dice onion celery and carrot. Slice zucchini, squash, and any other veggies desired. Peel and mince garlic. Lay aluminum foil onto a flat surface, shiny side up. Place each of the mixed ingredients into center of foil, add butter if not using ground beef, and fold foil up around ingredients to create a packet. Pinch shut and wrap entire packet in a second piece of foil, pinching that shut as well. Place foil packet directly into a low fire on or close to the coals. Cook for 20 minutes or until desired doneness is achieved.

❖   ❖   ❖   ❖

Lasagna

Equipment

Dutch Oven (with Lid)
Non-Stick Spray

Ingredients

1 pkg. no-boil lasagna noodles
1 jar red sauce or Alfredo sauce
4 oz. ricotta cheese
6 oz. grated mozzarella cheese
1 lb. ground beef (or ground pork, poultry, or sausage)
1 bunch fresh spinach
1 pkg. sliced mushrooms

Steps

For camping I recommend the no-cook noodles for this dish to make things easier. Spray your Dutch oven with non-stick spray. Spread a thin layer of sauce into the bottom of Dutch oven. Arrange noodles so that there is a single layer on top of the sauce, with little overlap and add a layer of sauce to the noodles. Next add a thin layer of meat, a layer of spinach and a light layer ricotta cheese. Finally, add a little mozzarella cheese then repeat layering process 4 or 5 times until noodles are almost are gone. Cover with a final layer of noodles; pour remaining sauce over noodles, and top with mozzarella. Cover Dutch oven and place onto heat. Cook at 350° with 25 coals with 17 on top and 8 on bottom and cook for 45 minutes.

❖   ❖   ❖   ❖

Mexican Lasagna

Equipment

Dutch Oven (with Lid)
Non-Stick Spray
(or Shortening)
Can Opener
Knife

Ingredients

1-2 cans re-fried beans
1-2 cans beef chili
1 jar salsa
4-6 large flour tortillas
1 lb. shredded cheddar cheese
(or Mexican blend)
1 package sour cream (optional)
1 package guacamole (optional)

Steps

Spray Dutch oven with non-stick spray or coat it with shortening. Spread a thin layer of salsa on the bottom to prevent the tortillas from sticking. Take a tortilla and spread a thin layer of re-fried beans on it. Place the bean-coated tortilla on the bottom of the Dutch oven Add a layer of chili (about ¼ can). Sprinkle lightly with salsa and spread cheese on the layer. Take a second tortilla and repeat the process until you have several layers. On the last layer, add extra salsa and sprinkle heavily with cheese. Cover Dutch oven and cook at about 375° using 34 coals with 22 on top and 12 on bottom for 30 to 45 minutes, or until heated throughout. Serve with sour cream and guacamole if desired.

❖   ❖   ❖   ❖

Sloppy Joes

Equipment

Knife
Cutting Board
Cast Iron Skillet
Spatula

Ingredients

1 c. green pepper
1 c. celery, finely chopped
1 c. onion, finely chopped
2 lbs. ground beef
2 c. barbecue sauce
2 c. water
2 tbsp. flour
1 tsp. salt

Steps

Chop green pepper, celery and onion and place them into skillet. Add ground beef, stir together, and cook over medium heat until meat is browned. Drain excess fat. Add remaining ingredients and simmer 20 to 25 minutes. Serve hot on toasted buns.

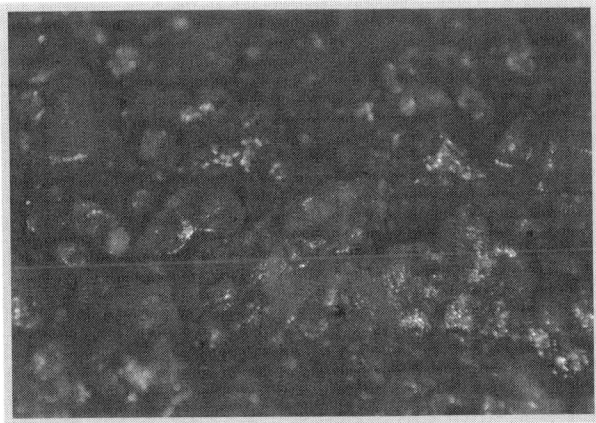

❖   ❖   ❖   ❖

Steak Recipes

Cooking steak is practically an art form. If you do it right then the steak is mouthwateringly wonderful. If you do it wrong you'll be chewing on either a piece of charred cardboard or a still mooing cow, or both at the same time when the heat is not even. Cooking steak is when heat control really comes into play - you must know what your heat is doing to get the best results.

I once had a friend cook steaks over a campfire. He didn't pay a lot of attention to how the heat was hitting the meat, and the result was steaks that were black on one side and still bloody rare on the other. Don't make this mistake. Think of the fire as you would any charcoal grill. A good, steady heat from evenly distributed coals is best, so start your fire at least an hour before you want to begin cooking and have ample coals when you are ready to start.

If you want to marinate your steaks you should do so for at least an hour before cooking, and whether you are cooking at home or around the campfire you should let the meat set out at room temp for at least 15 to 30 minutes prior to cooking. This will warm the meat closer to room temperature and help cook it more evenly.

Pat dry with a paper towel and add oil and a rub if desired. I sometimes add the rub a couple hours ahead of time to marinate, and keep the meat in a cooler until 15 to 30 minutes before cooking.

Once you have finished cooking your steak, be sure to let it rest for at least 5 minutes before cutting into it. This lets the juices, which are under pressure from the intense heat and moving quickly, settle. You will have a much juicier, tastier steak if you wait to dig in. Steaks can be either cooked in a skillet or put directly onto a grill grate for that that smoky campfire experience.

Cooking times vary with thickness. Here is a handy chart to help you determine the approximate length of time you wish to cook a piece of beef.

Beef Cooking Times Chart

Steaks ¾ inch thick or less

Rare (120°-130°) Cook 2 minutes each side.

Medium Rare (130°-140°) Cook 3 minutes each side.

Medium (140°-150°) Cook 4 minutes each side.

Medium Well (150°-160°) Cook 5 minutes each side.

For thicker steaks:

Thickness	1 Inch	1 1/4 Inches	1 3/4 Inches
Rare 120°-130°	8 min	10 min	12 min
Medium Rare 130°-140°	10 min	12 min	14 min
Medium 140°-150°	13 min	15 min	17 min
Medium Well 150°-160°	18 min	20 min	22 min

For each additional ¼ inch add 1 min

*All temperatures in *The Culinary Camper* are listed in Fahrenheit

**The U.S. Department of Agriculture (USDA) recommends cooking all whole cuts of meat to 145 °F as measured with a food thermometer placed in the thickest part of the meat, then allowing the meat to rest for three minutes before carving or consuming.

Beef Kabobs

Equipment

Knife
Cutting Board
Mixing Bowl
Metal Skewers (or Wood Skewers;
if you are using wood skewers you
should soak them in Potable Water
for at least 30 minutes before use)
Grill (optional)

Ingredients

2 sirloin steaks
1 sweet onion
2 bell peppers
6-8 small button mushrooms
6-8 cherry tomatoes
1 tsp. garlic salt
½ black pepper
1 tsp. olive oil

Steps

Cut steak, onion, and bell peppers into 1-2 inch cubes and place into mixing bowl. Add mushrooms and tomatoes. Sprinkle liberally with olive oil, garlic salt, and pepper. Add pieces to skewers, alternating between various ingredients. Repeat until skewers are full. Place skewers on grill or directly over flames (if your skewers are long enough) and cook for about 2 minutes, then flip and cook for another 2 minutes until desired doneness is reached.

❖   ❖   ❖   ❖

Camp Prime Rib

Equipment

Small Aluminum Drip Pan
Meat Thermometer (optional)
Tin Foil (optional)
Water
Platter
Plastic Wrap
Rotisserie
Rotisserie Forks (optional)

Ingredients

1 jar beef rub
(or any rub you prefer)
1 prime rib

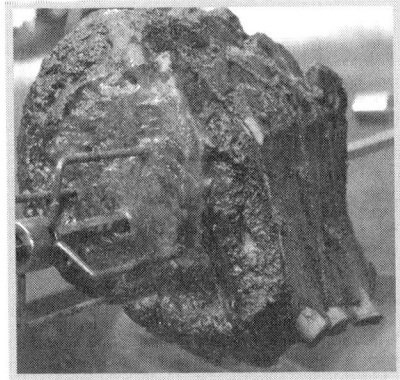

Steps

Coat the roast liberally with the rub, cover it with plastic wrap, and let it stand at room temperature for about an hour. After an hour, remove the wrap and slide the roast to the center of the rotisserie. I strongly recommend that you use rotisserie forks to help hold your meat in place while it turns.

Place the rotisserie over the fire. Place the aluminum drip pan onto the coals underneath the roast; this will provide diffused heat and reduce flare-ups from dripping grease. Cook for 15 minutes per pound. If you desire, check the internal temperature with a meat thermometer about a half hour before it should be done to ensure that it is reaching the correct medium-rare temperature of 125°-135°. If the roast seems to be cooking too slowly, you can place a loose cover of foil over the top of the rotisserie to keep the heat on the meat. You can also add more coals to the fire. If it seems to be cooking too quickly, sprinkle some water over the coals and drip pan.

*Roast pictured here with rotisserie forks. The roast was about seven and a half pounds (bone in) so it took just under 2 hours to cook. It was magnificent!

Filet Mignon with Bacon Sauce

Equipment

Basting Brush
Cutting Board
Knife
Aluminum Foil
Small Saucepan
Ladle or Large Spoon

Ingredients

4 - 4 oz. beef tenderloin filets
1 tsp. canola oil
3 slices bacon
1 tbsp. butter
4 shallots
¼ c. cream or half cream half milk
1 dash salt and pepper (to taste)

Steps

Brush grill grate lightly with canola oil or heat a cast iron pan with oil. Chop shallots and set aside. Chop bacon and set aside.

Brush filets with olive oil and sprinkle with salt and pepper. Cook on the grill to desired doneness (see **Beef Cooking Times Chart**, above). Plate the steaks and cover loosely with aluminum foil to rest. While the steaks are resting, cook the chopped bacon in a small saucepan over medium heat until the bacon pieces are crisp (approximately 3-5 minutes). Drain bacon grease and stir in the butter and shallots. Cook until the shallots are soft and translucent. Add the half-and-half and bring to a simmer over medium-low heat, stirring occasionally until the sauce is slightly thickened. Season the sauce to taste with salt and pepper and ladle over the steaks.

❖   ❖   ❖   ❖

Steak with Herbed Butter

Equipment

Knife
Cutting Board
Small Saucepan
Whisk (or Spoon)
Skillet
Grill
Basting Brush

Ingredients

1/2 c. butter
2 tsp. garlic powder
4 cloves garlic
1 tsp. dried basil
2 to 4 beef top sirloin or rib steaks
1 dash salt and pepper (to taste)

Steps

Peel and mince garlic. In a small saucepan, melt butter over medium-low heat with garlic powder, minced garlic, and basil. Set aside. Sprinkle both sides of each steak with salt and pepper. Move to grill and cook steaks to desired doneness (see **Beef Cooking Times Chart**, above in this chapter). When done, transfer to warmed plates. Immediately brush tops liberally with herbed butter, and let rest for 5 minutes before serving.

❖   ❖   ❖   ❖

Kalbe Marinated Flank Steak

Equipment

Cast Iron Frying Pan or
Grill Grate

Ingredients

2 flank steaks
1 tbsp. butter

Steps

Marinate beef steaks for 24 hours. Remove from marinade and grill for 7 minutes on each side. You can find my Kalbe marinade recipe in chapter 3 of this book.

❖   ❖   ❖   ❖

Steak on a Stick

Equipment

Knife
Cutting Board
Large Sealable Food Storage
Bag
Cooler
Ice
Metal Skewers
(or Wooden Skewers; if you
are using wooden skewers you
should soak them in Water for
at least 30 minutes before use)
Grill

Ingredients

2 lb. flank steak
1 tsp. fresh ginger
½ tsp. fresh garlic
½ c. soy sauce
¼ c. olive oil
¼ c. water
2 tbsp. molasses
2 tsp. mustard powder
½ tsp. onion powder
1 tsp. pepper

Steps

Cut steak into 4 to 6 inch long strips about 1 to 2 inches wide and set aside. Peel and mince garlic and mince ginger. In a large sealable food storage bag, combine the soy sauce, olive oil, water, molasses, mustard powder, ginger, garlic, onion powder, and pepper. Seal and shake the bag to mix ingredients together. Add steak strips to the bag and reseal.

Place into a cooler with ice and marinate for at about 8 hours.

About an hour before you are ready to cook, start your fire so you have a good bed of coals prepared. When the coals are ready, thread strips of steak onto skewers and place on the grill over the campfire. Cook for 3 to 4 minutes on each side.

❖ ❖ ❖ ❖

Cowgirl Rice

Equipment

Knife
Dutch Oven
Sauce Pan
Spoon

Ingredients

4 oz. beef jerky
2 tbsp. olive oil
¼ onion, finely chopped
1 cloves garlic, minced
1 tomato, chopped
1 cups rice
1 bay leaf
1 ½ c. water
1 tbsp. parsley
1 tbsp. basil
1 dash salt and pepper (to taste)

Steps

Soak the jerky in water for at least 2 hours. Remove jerky from water and cut into half inch cubes. Add water to Dutch oven and bring to a slow boil. Add onion and garlic and stir in jerky and tomato. Raise heat and cook another minute and add the rice, spices and bay leaf stirring to mix well. Cover and cook till rice is done and water is soaked up (depends on the type of rice used).

❖   ❖   ❖   ❖

7

Pork & Lamb

Baked Ham

This recipe will require that the ham fits insides your Dutch oven. Make sure your oven will accommodate the ham.

Equipment

Mixing Bowl
Spoon
Dutch Oven (or 2 heavy-duty disposable Aluminum Pans)
Aluminum Foil
Non-Stick Spray
Grill

Ingredients

1 lb. brown sugar
½ c. Dijon mustard
1 whole bone-in ham (12-15 lbs.)

Steps

In a mixing bowl, mix mustard and brown sugar until you have a thick paste. Set aside. Trim away excess fat from the ham. Lay a couple long pieces of foil out in a cross shape and center the ham on the foil. Spread the brown sugar/mustard paste thickly on top. Fold the foil up around the ham and pinch it closed; get as complete a seal as possible. If you are using the Dutch oven, spray the pan thoroughly with nonstick spray. Place the foil-wrapped ham into your Dutch oven, then cover. Bake with coals all around and on top so that it roasts approximately at a temperature of 350° using 25 coals with 17 on top and 8 on bottom for 4 hours. Do not open until ham is done. Let set with foil over the ham for about 20 minutes before serving.

❖   ❖   ❖   ❖

Baked Ham Ring

Equipment

Cooking Spray
Dutch Oven
Cutting Board
Knife

Ingredients

2¼ c. spinach (fresh)
¼ c. salami (optional)
¼ c. fresh parsley
1 onion (optional)
1 clove garlic
2 tubes pre-made crescent roll dough (8 count per tube)
1½ c. Swiss cheese (shredded; other cheese may be substituted)
¼ lb. boneless fully cooked ham (sliced)
2 tsp. mustard (yellow or Dijon)
1 tsp. lemon juice

Steps

Spray the inside of the Dutch oven with cooking spray. Unroll 1 tube crescent roll dough. The pieces will be triangular. Place triangles into the bottom a Dutch oven, narrow tips inward, so that the wide ends overlap, forming a circle. Lightly press the edges together to form a bottom crust.

Chop spinach, salami, ham, parsley and onion. Mince garlic. In a large bowl, combine all ingredients except dough. Spoon mixture into the center of the dough circle. Open the second tube of dough and unroll the triangles, laying them over the top of the ham mixture in the same pattern as before. Lightly pinch all the edges together to form a pie with the ham filling inside. Cover the Dutch oven and place it into the coals, baking at about 375° using 27 coals with 18 on top and 9 on bottom for 20-25 minutes or until golden brown.

Tip: Use a Dutch oven liner for this.

Be sure you don't burn the bottom.

❖   ❖   ❖   ❖

Cheesy Ham Casserole

Equipment

Water
Medium Saucepan
Cooking Spoon
Knife
Cutting Board
Colander
Large Mixing Bowl
Can Opener
Dutch Oven

Ingredients

1 pkg. spiral noodles
1 c. mushrooms
8 oz. ham
1 tbsp. shortening
(or other cooking grease)
2 cans condensed cream of
mushroom soup
3 tbsp. mayonnaise
2 c. sharp cheddar cheese
(shredded)
1½ c. parmesan cheese (grated)
Bread Crumbs

Steps

In a medium sauce pan bring about 3 quarts of water to boil, add the noodles and bring back to a boil, stirring occasionally. While the noodles boil, chop mushrooms and cube ham. In a large mixing bowl, stir together mushrooms, ham, soup, and cheddar cheese. Once the noodles are al dente, drain them well and stir them into the mixture. Lightly grease a Dutch oven or Dutch oven liner. Spread the mixture evenly into the Dutch oven and sprinkle with parmesan cheese and bread-crumbs. Cover, and bake in coals for 1 hour at about 375° using 27 coals with 18 on top and 9 on bottom, or until bubbly and lightly brown on top.

❖   ❖   ❖   ❖

Chops

Pork chops are cooked much like steak, and thickness is all-important when it comes to preparation. Thick cut chops do great when prepared with a brine, while thin cut chops (less than ¾ inch thick) are great with a marinade or just plain old salt and pepper. Rubs also work great for either thick or thin cut chops. If you use a brine, be sure to let the chops soak for about a couple hours. If you're using a rub, it should sit on the chops for at least 30 minutes before cooking. Barbeque sauce is also great with pork chops; the classic Carolina style sauce in chapter 3 works wonderfully.

Thin Cut Chops

Equipment

Aluminum Foil
Metal Spatula
Grill

Ingredients

2 pork chops
¼ tsp. garlic salt (to taste)
¼ tsp. pepper (to taste)
Or soak in pork brine or use rub

Steps

Start with a hot fire, and make sure your grill is ready to sizzle. Sprinkle your seasonings onto the chops on both sides. Place the chops on the grill. Cook for about 2 or 3 minutes then rotate the chops about a quarter turn and cook for about another 2 or 3 minutes. Flip the chops over and cook for 2 or 3 minutes then rotate a quarter turn and cook for another 2 minutes. Remove from heat. Overcooking a thin cut chop can result in a dry, flavorless piece of shoe leather, so be careful not to overdo it. Let the chops rest for about 5 minutes before serving.

Thick Cut Chops

Equipment

Aluminum Foil
Metal Spatula
Grill

Ingredients

2 pork chops (brined, seasoned, rubbed or however you prefer them)

Steps

Thick cut pork chops need a lower heat to cook all the way through but with longer cooking times. Build the fire up and place your grill over it. When the heat has died down place the chops on the grill, cover loosely with foil and cook for 8 minutes. Flip and cook for another 8 to 10 minutes covered loosely with the foil. Remove from heat and let rest on a plate covered with foil for 5 to 10 minutes before serving. Note: This will produce a medium rare chop. If you prefer a more done piece of pork increase the cooking time by 3 to 5 minutes on each side.

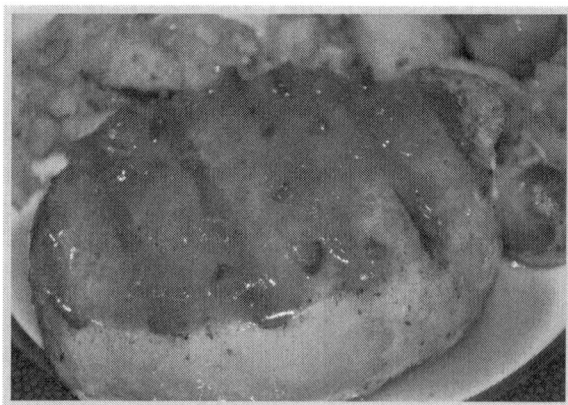

❖   ❖   ❖   ❖

Gouda Stuffed Pork Chops

Equipment

Cutting Board
Knife
Water
Basting Brush
Shallow Dish
(larger than the pork chops)
9x13 Inch Disposable
Aluminum Pan
Heavy-Duty Aluminum Foil
Grill

Ingredients

4 thick-cut pork chops
8 slices smoked Gouda cheese
1 bag fresh spinach
1 c. bread crumbs
3 tbsp. horseradish mustard
1 tbsp. Creole-style seasoning

Steps

Lay each chop flat on a cutting board, and carefully using a sharp knife held parallel to the board, cut a pocket into the pork, leaving three sides intact. Place a slice of smoked Gouda into each pocket.

Rinse the spinach well, dry and cut into bite-size pieces. Stuff each chop with spinach. Coat a disposable aluminum Dutch oven pan with cooking spray. Place breadcrumbs in a shallow dish. Brush each chop with a thin layer of mustard, roll in crumbs, and arrange in the pan. When all the stuffed chops are arranged, sprinkle with Creole seasoning and place in Dutch oven. Cover the Dutch oven with lid and place on heat. Bake for 25 minutes at 375° using 27 coals with 18 on top and 9 on bottom, or until brown and juices run clear.

❖　❖　❖　❖

Ham and Split Pea Soup

Equipment

Cutting Board
Knife
Large soup pot
Cooking Spoon
Ladle

Ingredients

2 tbsp. butter
½ onion
2 stalks celery
3 cloves garlic
1 lb. ham
1 bay leaf

1 lb. dried split peas
4 qt. chicken stock
(unsalted)
1 ham bone (optional)
1 tbsp. Salt (to taste)
1 pepper (to taste)

Steps

Chop the onion and celery and mince the garlic. Melt the butter in a large soup pot over medium-low heat. Stir in onion, celery, and minced garlic. Cook slowly for about 5 minutes. While that is heating, dice the ham. Add the ham, bay leaf, and split peas to the pot. Pour in chicken stock and stir (if using a left over ham bone be sure you have enough stock to cover the bone). Simmer slowly, stirring occasionally, until the peas are tender and the soup is thick, about an hour and a half to two hours depending on your peas.

❖   ❖   ❖   ❖

Kabobs

Equipment

Cutting Board
Knife
Small Mixing Bowl
Small Wire Whisk
(or small Spoon)
Plastic Sealable Food Storage
Bag
Skewers
Potable Water (if using
wooden skewers)
Basting Brush

Ingredients

2 lb. pork tenderloin
1 c. Teriyaki Marinade Sauce
2 tbsp. olive oil
1 can pineapple chunks (drained)
1 pint cherry tomatoes
2 red, green or yellow bell peppers

Steps

Chop pork tenderloin into 1 inch cubes and place into food storage bag; set aside. In a small mixing bowl, whisk together the teriyaki sauce and oil. Pour all but about ¾ c. of the mixture into the food storage bag with the pork cubes. Marinade meat in plastic bag for at least 1 hour.

While meat is marinating, soak skewers in water (if necessary). Cut peppers into 1 inch pieces. After meat has finished marinating, thread the meat onto the skewers, alternating between each cube with peppers, tomatoes and pineapple chunks. Place on grill 4 to 5 inches from heat. After 5 minutes, turn skewers over and brush with reserved marinade. Repeat after another 5 minutes have passed. Cook 5 more minutes or until done. Remove from heat, let stand 2 or 3 minutes and serve.

❖　❖　❖　❖

Lamb Stew

Equipment

Dutch Oven
(with Lid)
Potato Peeler
Knife
Cutting Board

Ingredients

8 medium red or Yukon potatoes
1 large onion
2 lb. boneless trimmed lamb shoulder
1 lb. mushrooms quartered
½ lb. thick-sliced bacon
1 tsp. thyme
2 tbsp. basil
3 tbsp. parsley
1 tsp. salt (to taste)
1 tsp. pepper (to taste)
5 c. lamb stock
1 bay leaf

Steps

Peel potatoes and slice into 1 inch cubes. Peel and quarter onions and then chop half of the quarters into pieces ½ inch thick and set aside. Dice bacon and set aside. Cut lamb into 1 inch cubes. Using the Dutch oven or a separate frying pan brown the lamb till just browned. Spread potatoes at bottom of Dutch oven. Layer ½ the onions on top of the potatoes. Layer lamb cubes & bacon over onions. Sprinkle seasonings onto meat. Cover with remaining potatoes and onions. Gently pour in the stock. Sprinkle top with more salt and pepper, and toss in bay leaf. Cover and cook at 350° using 25 coals with 17 on top and 8 on bottom for 2½ hours. Remove bay leaf before serving. Alternatively you can do this over a stove with a large stew pot.

❖   ❖   ❖   ❖

Pulled Pork

Pull apart the roast after it has cooled for at least an hour.

Equipment

Dutch Oven with Rack
Tongs
Meat Thermometer

Ingredients

1 pork shoulder roast
2 - 4 tbsp. rub (of your choice)

I like to sear the meat first before roasting. Searing meat over high heat creates a delicious browned crust due to what's called the Maillard reaction. I like to sear the meat in a Dutch oven, then place a rack in the oven and finish slow-cooking the meat in that. Why dirty another pan just to cook the same piece of meat. Make sure to use a rack or the meat cooks in too much of its own fat or may stick to the bottom.

Steps

Liberally rub the roast and let set at room temperature for about 30 minutes. To sear the roast, get the Dutch oven good and hot and sear the meat on each side for about 4 minutes.

Place the roast fatty side up; the fat will drip down and baste the meat as it cooks, keeping it juicy and tender. Insert the meat thermometer into the center of the roast and cover with the lid.

Maintain a cooking temperature of about 225° using 15 coals with 11 on top and 4 on bottom. You will need to cook the meat for several hours, so be prepared to add fuel and monitor the temperature of your meat. You will definitely want to use a meat thermometer. The desired temperature you want your roast to reach internally is 165°-170°, do not let the internal temp to go above 190°. Check internal temperature at least once an hour until internal temperature has reached 165°-170°. Remove the roast from the heat and let cool for an hour.Pull roast apart with a fork, season meat with BBQ sauce and serve as is or on a bun.

❖   ❖   ❖   ❖

Ribs

Equipment

Butter Knife
Dutch Oven
Cooler with Ice (optional)
Meat Thermometer
(optional)

Ingredients

1 to 2 p. pork ribs
1 tbsp. vegetable oil
2 tbsp. pork rub
2 tbsp. barbeque sauce

Steps

First remove the membrane of the ribs by inserting a butter knife to loosen the membrane from the backside of the ribs, then reach in with your fingers to pull it up and remove it. If you do it right you can just peel the whole membrane off in one swoop. Next, rub the meat with a little oil and apply your spice rub to both sides. Set the ribs into a Dutch oven with a rack to keep them out of the grease and cover with lid.

The ribs should cook at around 225° using 15 coals with 11 on top and 4 on bottom for about 2 to 4 hours for baby back ribs, or 3 or 5 hours for larger ribs. You should begin checking the ribs for doneness after about 2 hours. If the meat is falling off the bone the ribs are definitely done, but you can use a meat thermometer to be sure. The meat's internal temperature should be 175°-180°.

Once the ribs are done, remove the pan and stoke the fire lightly so that you have a small hot flame. Slap some barbeque sauce onto the meat and place it back over the flame to caramelize a bit. Cook for about 3 minutes over this high heat. Only coat the meat once, your friends and family can add more if they like. Serve with coleslaw, corn on the cob and/or baked beans.

❖ ❖ ❖ ❖

Pork Shoulder Roast

Equipment

Knife
Rotisserie
Basting Brush
Meat Thermometer

Ingredients

1 pork shoulder (about 4 Lb.)
10 cloves garlic (peeled)
1 bottle Dijon mustard

Steps

With the tip of a sharp knife, make small 1 inch deep slits all over the surface of the roast. Insert sliced cloves of garlic into the slits. Place roast onto the rotisserie and baste all over with mustard. Set over a low fire, turning a quarter turn about every 30 minutes, for about 3 hours, or until roast reaches about 160° internal temperature. Remove from the fire and let rest for at least 20 minutes before carving.

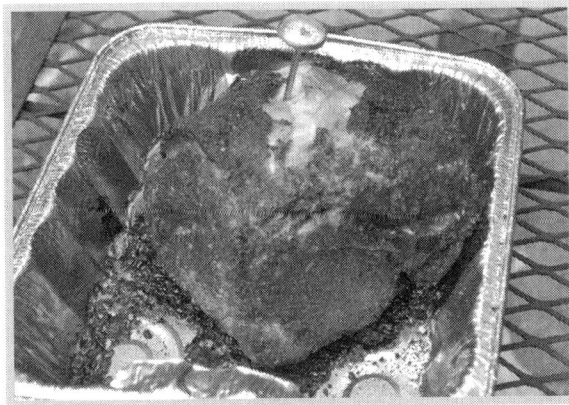

❖   ❖   ❖   ❖

Stuffed Portobello Mushrooms

Equipment

Dutch Oven
(or Cast Iron Skillet with Lid)
Cutting Board
Knife
Mixing Bowl
Spoon

Ingredients

1 lb. ground spicy Italian sausage
2 - 4 Portobello mushrooms
1 red bell pepper
1 c. fresh spinach

Steps

Wash mushrooms and remove stems. Chop stems somewhat finely and set aside. With a spoon, clean out the mushroom caps by removing the black gills, being careful not to break the mushroom. Wash bell pepper and chop into small pieces. Place sausage, mushroom stems and peppers in a bowl and mix together well. Fill caps with the sausage mixture and place into Dutch oven. Cover and cook at about 375° using 27 coals with 18 on top and 9 on bottom for about 35 minutes.

❖ ❖ ❖ ❖

Tenderloin

Equipment

Cast Iron Pan

Ingredients

½ c. olive oil
2 lb. pork tenderloin

Steps

Coat the Tenderloin with oil. Place the tenderloin into the heated cast iron pan and cook around 9 or 10 minutes per side (depending on thickness) or until the meat reaches an internal temperature of 165° and juices run clear. Let the pork rest for 10 minutes then serve. Optional serve with a sauce or herbed butter. Pictured here is a tenderloin piece served with Carolina barbeque sauce

❖   ❖   ❖   ❖

Bobbi's Bitchen' Enchiladas

Equipment

Cooking Spray
Knife (optional)
Cutting Board (optional)
Can Opener
Mixing Bowl
Cooking Spoon
Dutch Oven

Ingredients

2 10 oz. can enchilada sauce
4-5 c. grated cheese (cheddar,
Monterey jack , or mozzarella)
2-3 c. pre-cooked ground pork,
shredded or pulled pork
1 pkg. corn or flour tortillas
1 avocado (optional)
1 jar salsa (optional)

Steps

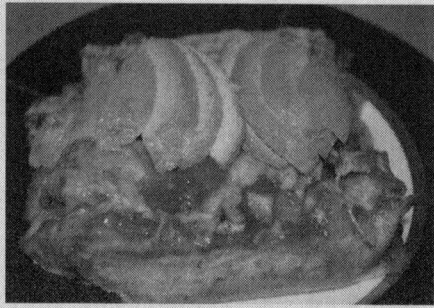

Spray tortillas on both sides with a small amount of cooking spray. Place them, stacked, into Dutch oven; cover, and set over low heat to warm.

Cut or pull apart the meat into small pieces. In a mixing bowl, mix together 1 can enchilada sauce with 3-4 c. grated cheese and 2-3 c. meat.

Remove Dutch oven from heat and remove tortillas. Spray inside of Dutch oven lightly with cooking spray. Place enchilada mixture into tortillas, roll tortillas and place in Dutch oven. Pour other can of sauce over rolled enchiladas. Sprinkle with remaining cheese.

Cover Dutch oven and bake at 350° using 25 coals with 17 on top and 8 on bottom for 20-25 minutes. Serve with sliced avocado and salsa if desired. If you prefer less sauce and cheese, reduce amount given by one cup or amount desired.

Pizza

Equipment

Knife
Cutting Board
Dutch Oven
Heavy Duty Oven Mitts

Ingredients

1 ready-made (or homemade)
pizza crust
1 can tomato paste
(or 1 can pizza sauce)
2 c. mozzarella cheese (to taste)
1 package Italian pork sausage
1 c. sliced mushrooms
1 tsp basil (to taste)
1 tsp. oregano (to taste)
1 tbsp. garlic (to taste)
1 tsp. Italian seasoning (to taste)

Steps

If necessary, shape or trim pizza crust to fit your Dutch oven. In a mixing bowl, combine tomato paste with spices; spread on top of the pizza dough. Sprinkle a small amount of cheese on the pie to create a base for your toppings. This will help keep the toppings from slipping off the pie. Next, add the toppings of sausage and mushroom. Finally, add your desired amount of cheese to the top of the pizza.

Bake at 400° using 29 coals with 19 on top and 10 on bottom for 15 minutes. Check after 15 minutes that the dough is cooked and the cheese is melted. Let sit for 2 minutes before serving.

I have also used pre-baked artisan breads as a pizza base as in the photo below. This method makes it easy to create pizza when camping. Once you have added sauce, toppings and cheese to the bread, simply wrap it loosely in foil, creating a sort of tent over the top keeping the foil away from the cheese, and set the packet in indirect heat, turning if necessary, until cheese is melted. Once the cheese has melted its ready to eat.

❖   ❖   ❖   ❖

8

Fish & Seafood

Beer-Poached Trout

I've been on a couple of camping trips where we unexpectedly caught trout and wanted to cook it right away while it was fresh. The problem was we had no butter or oil in which to cook it. Being young and thirsty, though, we had beer, so we improvised with this tasty recipe. You could probably do this with water instead, but beer gives the fish a really nice flavor.

Equipment

Skillet
Spatula

Ingredients

2 fresh trout (see the appendix for How to Gut and Clean Fish)
½ to 1 can beer
½ tsp. salt
½ tsp. pepper

Steps

To make fish this way just pour some beer into your skillet and toss some spices in if you have any. Bring beer to a low simmer over medium-high heat. Once the beer is simmering, add your fish and cook for about 5 minutes on each side. Remove from heat and sprinkle with salt and pepper. Serve immediately.

Red Neck Fish Wrap

Equipment

Knife
Cutting Board
Mixing Bowl
Shallow Plate or Dish
Cast Iron Pan
Spatula
Aluminum Foil
(or clean towel)
Cooking Spoon (optional)

Ingredients

1 can sliced olives
1 fresh tomato
1 c. romaine lettuce
1 tbsp. ranch dressing
1 filet halibut, bass or any white fish (See appendix for How to Gut and Clean Fish)
1 tsp. blackened or Creole seasoning (see Chapter 3 or choose your own blackened seasoning.)
2 tbsp. olive oil
2 to 4 tortillas (corn or flour)

Steps

Chop or tear lettuce into bite sized pieces and dice tomato. In a large mixing bowl mix together lettuce, tomatoes, olives and ranch dressing; set aside.

Wash fish and pat dry. Rub fish pieces lightly with olive oil. Place blackened seasoning in a shallow plate or dish. Coat both sides of fish pieces evenly with seasoning. Heat olive oil in a cast iron frying pan at a medium high temperature; when oil is hot add fish to pan. Cook for 3 to 4 minutes on each side and remove.

Prep tortillas by spraying each with a little non-stick spray and heating them in a frying pan. Contrary you can spray each tortilla with non-stick spray and stack the tortillas on a piece of foil. Wrap the foil and place over heat for several minutes until warm. Cut a small strip of fish, add it to a warm tortilla, add some of the salad mixture, wrap and serve.

❖   ❖   ❖   ❖

Cedar Plank Salmon

I made this dish on the Washington coast after coming back from a fishing charter trip with several large salmon. I wanted to cook the fish right away since it was so fresh, so I experimented with this over a campfire and it turned out fabulously.

Equipment

Cedar Plank
Water
Paper Towel

Ingredients

2 salmon fillets (See appendix for How to Fillet Fish)
1 cedar grilling plank
1 tbsp. olive oil
1 tsp. seafood rub

Steps

For this recipe, you need to make sure your fire is low and the coals are deep and hot, so start it at least an hour prior to cooking. Soak the cedar planks in water for at least 15 minutes. Rinse fish, pat dry with a paper towel, and place (skin side down) on soaked cedar planks. Sprinkle olive oil on fish and either rub or sprinkle with desired seafood spices. Place the plank on the fire grate making sure that the fire only lightly kisses the plank. Cook the salmon for 8-10 minutes or until fish is medium rare or medium. If you overcook the fish it will be dry, but if you remove it from the heat once it has reached medium rare the fish will continue cooking for a bit afterward and will be perfectly cooked after a few minutes.

❖ ❖ ❖ ❖

Clam Chowder

Equipment

Cutting Board
Knife
Grater
Dutch oven
(or Soup Pot)
Cooking Spoon

Ingredients

3-4 slices bacon
1-2 large carrot
1 large onion
2 cloves garlic
2-3 medium Yukon
potatoes
¼ c. butter
1 tsp. marjoram
2 tsp. basil
2 tsp. oregano
1 tsp. thyme
2 tsp. dill
1 tsp. sage

2 tsp. parsley
2 c. clam juice
2 tbsp. flour
1½ c. cream, half and
half
(or whole milk)
½ lb. fresh clams (or
¼ lb. canned)
1 tsp. salt (to taste)
1 tsp. pepper (to taste)
1 tsp hot sauce
(optional)

Steps

Chop bacon and cook over low heat for 5 to 10 minutes in Dutch oven or large soup pan. The bacon doesn't need to get crispy. While the bacon is cooking, dice or grate the carrots and chop both the onion and garlic fine. Slice the potatoes ¼ to ½ inch thick. Add the butter, spices and clam juice to the pot. Slowly whisk in the flour and bring to a boil. Add the potatoes, onions and garlic and let simmer. After 10 or 15 minutes, reduce heat. Add the half and half and cook another 10 minutes without boiling the broth. Add the clams and cook another 2 minutes. Add salt and pepper to taste. If you like your clam chowder with a little kick, you can add a dash of hot sauce. Serve immediately with bread or oyster crackers.

❖   ❖   ❖   ❖

Fresh Crab

Growing up on the west coast gave us an abundance of fresh crab, and not just any crab but Dungeness crab, which to my mind is one of the tastiest crabs in the world. My father used to take us ocean fishing a lot and we would always take the crab net with us. Even if you are not catching it yourself, you should always use live crab. If you buy crab that is dead you should probably not eat it and toss it. Really, do not settle. Eating bad seafood will be something you remember for a very long time and not in a pleasant way.

Equipment

Large Stock Pot (or Steamer)
Tongs
Pail (or deep pan)
Ice
Water
Small Saucepan
Whisk
Cutting Board
Knife
Shellfish Crackers

Ingredients

2 -4 live crab
8 qt. water
½ stick butter (per serving)
1 tsp. garlic powder (per serving)
1 lemon

Steps

Crab can be either steamed or boiled; it really depends on the equipment you have. If you have a large enough steamer then you may prefer to steam it, but I have to say I've always boiled my crab. This also brings up the question of whether to boil it live. Some people find this cruel, so if you prefer not to live boil you can take a heavy blunt object and hit the crab sharply on the head to knock it out or kill it first. If you plan to cook your crab live you can put it on ice for about a half an hour immediately prior to cooking to slow the crab down and make it easier to handle. Get your water/steamer boiling hot, then add the crab. Cook the crab for about 7 or 8 minutes per pound.

Once the crab is cooked, place it under cool water to stop the cooking process. When camping I use a large pan with ice water.

See the Appendix for how to clean crab

❖   ❖   ❖   ❖

Lobster

Being from the west coast we don't have fresh lobster very often so this is not something that gets done over a camp fire where I'm from. The west coast does however have Cray fish and what are Cray fish but tiny little lobster. I've fished for and eaten a lot of Cray fish using this method.

Equipment

Large Stock Pot (or Steamer)
Tongs
Pail (or deep pan)
Ice & Water

Small Saucepan
Whisk
Cutting Board
Knife
Shellfish Crackers

Ingredients

2 – 4 live lobster or 1 to 2 pounds of Cray fish
8 qt. water
½ stick butter (per serving)
1 tsp. garlic powder (per serving)
1 lemon

Steps

Lobster can also be steamed or boiled just like crab. Again, if you plan to cook your lobster live you can put it on ice for about a half an hour immediately prior to cooking to slow the lobster down and make it easier to handle. Get your water/steamer boiling hot, then add the lobster for about 7 or 8 minutes per pound. Once the lobster is cooked, place it under cool water to stop the cooking process.

Remove the tail section by gripping the chest in one hand and the tail in the other and twist clockwise to break the tail off of the chest. Remove the meat from the tail and eat. Twist off the claws and legs and crack with a hammer or pliers. There is also meat in the chest section. Cut the chest in half with strong scissors and pull out stomach and discard. Inside the chest you will find a maze of small pockets enclosing little nuggets of lobster meat. This meat is difficult to get to but is said to be some of the best meat on the lobster if you are patient enough to dig for it.

❖   ❖   ❖   ❖

Fresh Shrimp

Equipment

Cutting Board
Knife
Skillet (or Saucepan)
Spatula

Ingredients

1 lemon
1 lb. cleaned shrimp (See appendix for How to Clean Shrimp)
2 tbsp. butter (or 1 tbsp. olive oil and 1 tbsp. butter)
1 tsp. garlic powder

Steps

Clean the shrimp and devein. Slice lemon into quarters; set aside. Over medium heat, melt 1 tbsp. butter or olive oil in a skillet. Once the oil or butter is hot add the shrimp and cook for about 3 or 4 minutes depending on how hot your pan is. Shrimp cooks very quickly; once it turns opaque all the way through it is done. Once the shrimp is cooked, plate it and set aside. In the same saucepan you just used, melt the remaining butter. Add garlic powder and the juice from ¼ lemon to the butter, whisk over low heat for 1 more minute, and drizzle over the top of the shrimp or poor into a dipping cup.

❖   ❖   ❖   ❖

Fresh Trout

Equipment

Cutting Board
Knife
Skillet
Spatula

Ingredients

1 lemon
1 tsp. dill (fresh or dried)
2 fresh trout (see appendix for
How to Gut and Clean Fish)
½ tsp. garlic salt
2 tbsp. olive oil

Steps

Slice the lemon very thin, and chop the dill finely if necessary. Sprinkle some dill inside the fish and place the lemon slices inside as well. Heat up a cast iron skillet over medium-high heat and add 2 tbsp. olive oil to the pan. Once the pan is hot add trout. Sear the trout for about 2 to 3 minutes. Turn and cook for another 2 to 3 minutes. The fish skin should be crispy on each side. Remove from pan, drizzle with some more olive oil and sprinkle with a little garlic salt.

❖   ❖   ❖   ❖

Fried Razor Clams

Equipment

Mixing Bowl
Wire Whisk
Cast Iron Skillet
Plates (or low
sided Bowls)
Tongs (or
Spatula)
Paper Towels

Ingredients

3 eggs (for 15 clams)
1 tsp. paprika
1 tsp. Chili Powder
1 tsp. Garlic Powder
1 lb. Razor Clams
(shelled and cleaned; see
appendix for How to
Clean Razor Clams)

2 c. flour
1 c. canola oil
(amount varies with
size of skillet)

Steps

Whisk the eggs well and set aside. Add seasonings to the flour and mix well. Add about ¼ inch of Canola oil to a cast iron skillet and set over medium high heat. Now place 1 c. flour mixture onto one plate and the remaining onto another separate shallow plate. Dredge the clams in one of the plates of flour (this assures that the egg sticks to the clams), then the egg, and finally in the second plate of flour, making sure the clams are thoroughly coated. When all the clams are ready, place them into the pan of hot oil. Cook for about 1 to 2 minutes, turn and cook another 1 minute, making sure the clams are brown on each side. Remove from the oil and set on paper towels to absorb excess oil. Serve with tartar or cocktail sauce for dipping.

❖   ❖   ❖   ❖

Key Lime Sea Bass

Equipment

Potable Water
Shallow Bowl
Cooking Spoon
Aluminum Foil
Grill

Ingredients

4 - 4 to 6 oz. sea bass fillets
½ c. mayonnaise
1 tsp. dill
1 tsp. garlic powder
2 small key limes (juiced)
½ tsp. salt (to taste)
½ tsp. pepper (to taste)

Steps

Wash the fillets and make sure all bones have been removed. Mix mayonnaise, dill, garlic, lime juice, salt and pepper together in a shallow bowl. Place a large piece of aluminum foil on the table, shiny side up. Dip a fillet into the mayonnaise mixture, coating it thickly, and place onto the center of the foil. Repeat for each fillet. Wrap each in a piece of foil loosely around the fillets and place them on a grill over medium heat for about 10 to 15 minutes. (For very thin fillets this time should be lowered.)

❖　　❖　　❖　　❖

Nana Tidwell's Salmon Pie

This is another one of my mother's recipe's that she liked quite a bite. I felt a need to include several of my mother's favorites in memory of her. Plus she was a great cook.

Equipment

Dutch Oven
Cast Iron Skillet
(with Lid)
Cutting Board
Knife
Small Mixing
Bowl
Wire Whisk
Oven Mitts

Ingredients

1 pre-baked pie
crust (cooled; can be
done at home)
1½ c. grated ched-
dar cheese
3 tbsp. flour
1 lb. fresh salmon
(see appendix for
How to Fillet Salmon)

2 tbsp. butter
1 bunch green onions
1 can cream of mush-
room soup
¾ c. sour cream
1 tsp. dill
½ tsp. pepper
2 eggs

Steps

Pre bake the pie crust in a cast iron pan with a lid, but leave ample time for it to cool for this recipe. When the crust is sufficiently cool, spread half the cheese around the bottom of the pie crust. Place the pie crust into the Dutch oven and set aside. Cut salmon into 1 inch cubes. Chop onions and set aside. Lightly beat eggs and set aside. Mix salmon with flour just to coat slightly and add to pie shell. In the skillet, melt butter over low heat; add onions and sauté until softened. Raise heat, add the soup, sour cream, dill, pepper, and eggs and stir until it just boils. Remove from heat and let cool slightly. Pour mixture over salmon and add the remaining cheese to the top. Cover Dutch oven bake at 325° using 23 coals with 16 on top and 7 on bottom for 20 to 25 minutes.

❖　❖　❖　❖

Salmon Steaks

Equipment

Skillet or grill

Ingredients

1 tsp. dill
1 tsp. salt
1 tsp. pepper

Steps

Cut the salmon cross ways through the bone or you can buy the steaks already cut. Lightly coat the salmon with olive oil and sprinkle with dill, salt and pepper. Grill on each side for about 5 minutes depending on how think the steaks are.

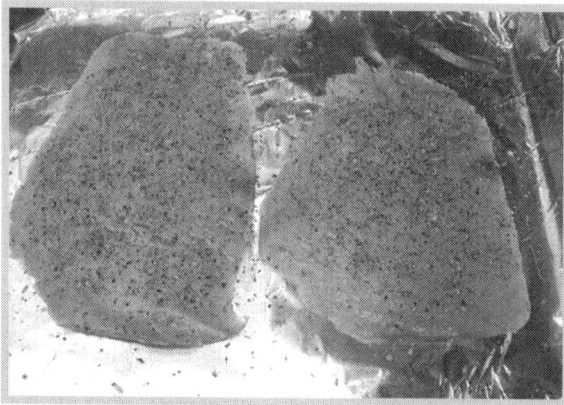

❖   ❖   ❖   ❖

Shanna Montana's Fantastic Mountain Trout

Equipment

Knife
Cutting Board
Fish Scaler
Potable Water
Aluminum Foil
Tongs (or Hand Protection)

Ingredients

1/3 small zucchini (per serving)
¼ small onion (per serving)
2 whole fish (fish of your choice; see appendix for How to Gut and Clean Fish)

1 tbsp. butter (or olive oil)
1 tsp. dill
½ tsp. Tarragon
1 tsp. Garlic Powder
1 tsp. salt (to taste)
½ tsp. Pepper (to taste)

Steps

Slice zucchini and onion thinly and set aside. Remove scales from fish and rinse well. Smear the skin with butter or olive oil. Sprinkle dill, garlic and tarragon outside and inside fish. Stuff the inside with zucchini and onion slices. Add salt and pepper if desired. Wrap fish in individual pieces of tin foil, pinching foil tightly shut, and toss directly onto a low fire or near the coals of a hot fire.

Cook for about 10 minutes or to your desired doneness (remember fish can cook very quickly depending on thickness and heat levels). Remove from fire with tongs or hand protection. Open the foil carefully; there will likely be a burst of very hot steam when the foil is opened. Shanna likes to serve this with rice and/or a medley of roasted root veggies.

This recipe and the recipe for Shanna's Hobo Stew are courtesy of my friend Shanna Montana.

❖   ❖   ❖   ❖

Steamed Clams or Mussels

I've been fortunate to have lived my whole life close to an ocean and close to some fantastic seafood. One of my favorite childhood memories is of my parents serving up fresh steamed clams just like this at the end of a sun-soaked day at the beach, and I know you'll enjoy these just as much as I did back then.

Equipment

Large Shallow Dish
Steamer*
Knife
Cutting Board
Small Saucepan
Wire Whisk

Ingredients

3-5 lbs. live clams or mussels
2 c. water (cold)
1 Walla Walla sweet onion
1 tsp. parsley (dried or fresh)
¼ c. white wine (optional)

1 loaf fresh bread
½ stick butter (per serving)
½ tsp. garlic powder (per serving)
1 tsp. lemon juice (per serving)

*or create one by propping a bowl or a metal strainer inside of a larger pot; your larger pot must have a tightly fitting lid.

Steps

Soak clams in cold water for about 1/2 hour until they spit out any sand they may be holding. Place about 2 cups of water into the steamer and set onto high heat. While the water is heating, chop fresh parsley and ½ of the onion. Once the water has begun to boil, place clams into the steamer and add the parsley and onion on top of the clams. Cover, and steam clams for about 5 minutes or until the clams have opened at least a half inch. Be sure not to overcook or you will be chewing on little nuggets of rubber. In a small saucepan, melt butter over low heat. Add garlic powder, lemon juice and wine (if desired) and whisk briefly. Serve with bread. The water from the steamer can be served as broth along with the clams if desired.

If steaming mussels be sure to soak in cold water to remove sand. Wash the mussels thoroughly and brush the shells to remove encrusted sand. Be sure to remove the beards left on the mussels from harvesting. Once the mussels are cleaned you can steam them the same way you steam clams.

Note: Please heed any shell fish warnings before harvesting mussels, oysters or clams and check beach regulations for consumption safety.

Also note that if a clam or mussel does not open during steaming toss it out. It is probably bad and should not be pried open and eaten.

❖　❖　❖　❖

Grilled Oysters

Equipment

Grill Grate
Tongs

Ingredients

1 – 2 lbs oysters
1 lemon juice squeezed
1 tbsp melted butter
1 tsp. hot sauce (to taste)

Steps

Soak oysters in cold water for 10 minutes, scrub off any debris from the shells. Place the oysters in the entire shell on the grill grate and cook until the oysters open. They should steam inside the shell before they open up. Sprinkle with lemon juice, melted butter and/or hot sauce and serve warm.

Note: Please head any shell fish warnings before harvesting mussel's oysters or clams and check beach regulations for consumption safety.

❖   ❖   ❖   ❖

Pan Fried Sea Bass (or any white fish)

Equipment
Cast Iron Frying Pan
Spatula
Small Sauce Pan

Ingredients
2 lbs fresh sea bass
½ tsp. garlic powder
½ tsp. onion powder
½ tsp. paprika
¼ tsp. chili pepper

¼ tsp. pepper
½ tsp. salt
3 tbsp. butter
1 tbsp. olive oil
1 tsp. lemon juice

Steps

Mix all the seasonings in a small bowl and generously sprinkle mixture on both sides of the fish. Slowly melt the butter in the sauce pan. While the butter is melting heat the frying pan to a medium heat with olive oil. Add the seasoned fish and cook for about 6 or 7 minutes, turn and brush cooked side with a little of the melted butter. Cook another 6 or 7 minutes, remove from heat and place on a plate. Brush more butter on the fish before serving.

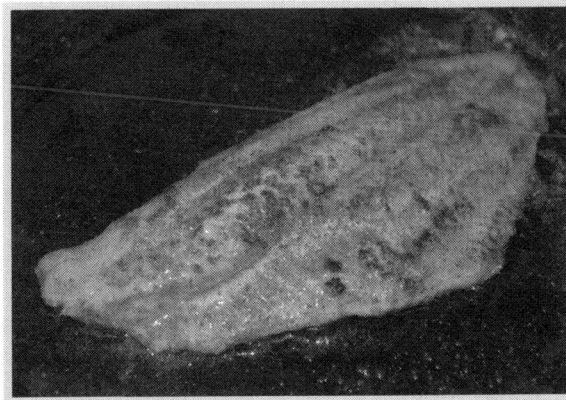

❖   ❖   ❖   ❖

Fish Tacos

Tacos are an extremely versatile food that can be adapted to almost any ingredient, and my favorite tacos are fish tacos.

Equipment

Cutting Board
Knife
Small Bowl
Shallow Baking Dish
Non-Stick Spray
Tin foil
Grill

Ingredients

1 red onion
1 to 2 c. red wine vinegar
1 to 2 lbs. fresh white fish (I recommend Mahi Mahi or Halibut)
1 lemon
1 tsp. dill
½ head shredded cabbage (or iceberg lettuce)
1 tomato (diced)

1 package tortillas (corn or flour; or crispy taco shells)
1 bottle taco sauce (or homemade)
½ lbs. grated cheese (cheddar, Monterey jack, or Mexican)
1 jar salsa (optional)
1 avocado (optional)

Steps

Start a fire so that it will be ready to grill in about a half hour to grill the fish. Alternatively you can pan fry the fish over a stove. Peel red onion and chop into ½ inch pieces or smaller. Place pieces into small bowl and add enough red wine vinegar to completely cover them.

Marinate fish in the shallow baking dish with lemon and dill for about 30 minutes. While the fish and onions are marinating, chop cabbage and tomatoes and set aside.

If you are using soft tortillas, spray each side with a little non-stick spray, then stack and wrap in foil. Place the tortillas onto the grill off to the side to warm. Grill fish and remove from grill after 8 to

10 minutes depending on the thickness of the fish. Remove red onions from the vinegar.

To assemble, cut the fish into strips about an inch thick, and place a piece or two in the center of each tortilla. Next, add about a tbsp. of taco sauce or red onions, then add cabbage, tomato, cheese and avocado, and serve.

Note: You can also make this recipe with fried fish instead of grilled; beer-battered fish is very tasty.

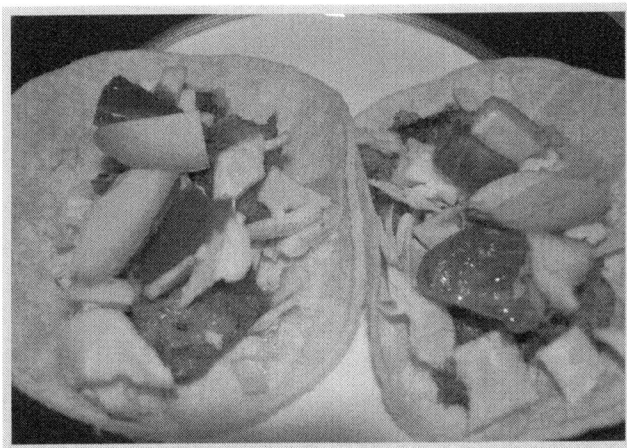

❖   ❖   ❖   ❖

Tuna Casserole

Equipment

Large Saucepan
(or Stock Pot)
2 Qt. Water
Cooking Spoon
Colander
Dutch Oven
(with Lid)

Ingredients

1 - 12 oz. pkg. egg noodles
4 cloves garlic
(or less if you prefer)
3 - 5 oz. cans tuna (drained)
2 - 5 oz. cans minced clams (drained)
2 cans condensed cream of mushroom soup
1 c. milk

8 oz. peas (frozen, or canned and drained; optional)
8 oz. corn (frozen, or canned and drained; optional)
½ c. bread crumbs
1 tbsp. paprika
1 c. cheddar Cheese (shredded; to taste)
2 tsp. salt
1 tsp. pepper

Steps

Cook and drain noodles to al dente and add to Dutch oven. Peel and mince garlic. Add garlic, tuna, clams, cream of mushroom soup, milk, and peas or corn (if desired) to Dutch oven; mix well. Sprinkle with breadcrumbs and paprika. Cover Dutch oven with lid and place directly into coals, adding coals to the top as well. Cook for 20-25 minutes at around 400° using 29 coals with 19 on top and 10 on bottom. Serve with some shredded cheese and salt and pepper to taste.

❖   ❖   ❖   ❖

Grilled Catfish

Equipment

Wire Grill

Ingredients

2 lbs. catfish
2 tsp. blackened seasoning
1 tsp. salt (if desired)
1 fresh lemon wedge

Steps

Pat dry the catfish filets and light coat with olive oil. Sprinkle on spices. Cook over grill for 6 to 9 minutes depending thickness of fish. Serve with a wedge of lemon.

❖   ❖   ❖   ❖

Seared Ahi Tuna

Equipment

Cast Iron Frying Pan

Ingredients

1 lb sushi grade yellow fin tuna steak
1 tsp. salt
1 tsp. pepper
1 tbsp. garlic bread crumbs
3 tbsp. butter
1 tbsp. olive oil

Steps

Heat cast iron pan to a medium high heat and melt the butter with the oil in the pan. Season the tuna with salt and pepper. Spread bread crumbs in a shallow dish and coat each tuna steak in the bread crumbs. Place the tuna in the pan and sear for 1 ½ to 2 minutes on each side.

❖   ❖   ❖   ❖

9
Dessert

This camping recipe book would not be complete without a list of desserts to make around the fire. This is a fun time for families and friends to experience bonding and kids love this part of the camping trip. If you let your kids cook around the fire please be sure to educate them on safety tips. As I write this I am reminded of my days as a camp counselor when I would tell my kids not to wave a flaming marshmallow on that stick as it may fly off and hit someone. Blowing on the flame will put it out much more efficiently and also save people from any serious flaming marshmallow burns.

S'mores

S'mores are a camping staple. Here I've listed the classic S'more recipe along with a couple of tricks I've learned over the years.

Equipment

Marshmallow Roasting Stick

Ingredients

1 bag large marshmallows
1 package chocolate bars
1 package graham crackers

Steps

The traditional way to make S'mores is to take a graham cracker half, place a piece of the chocolate bar on one side, put a roasted marshmallow on top of the chocolate, and place the other half of the graham cracker over the marshmallow. Let it stand for about a minute to get the chocolate to melt then eat.

Another way I like to make S'mores is to put the marshmallow in the middle of the chocolate and graham cracker and place it on one side of the pie iron. Close up the pie iron and roast over the fire. This will give you a nicely melted marshmallow along with the chocolate and the added bonus is that the graham cracker is slightly toasted and warm. Very tasty!

❖   ❖   ❖   ❖

S'more-E-O's

This recipe was submitted to this book by my friend Mackenzie. This is a man who lives for sweats and loves his cookies.

Equipment

Marshmallow Roasting Stick

Ingredients

1 bag of large marshmallows
1 package chocolate bars
1 package chocolate sandwich cookies

Steps

The steps are the same as for classic S'mores, the only difference is you use cream filled cookies instead of graham crackers. You can also you other kinds of cookies if you wish. I've made this recipe with chocolate chip cookies and the results were amazing.

❖   ❖   ❖   ❖

Peanut Butter S'mores

Equipment

Marshmallow Roasting Stick

Ingredients

1 bag large marshmallows
1 package peanut butter cup candy
1 package graham crackers

Steps

The steps are the same as for classic S'mores, the only difference is you use a peanut butter cup instead of the chocolate bar.

The last variation of the S'more recipe is to use cookies and peanut butter cup to create your S'more. I also prefer to use chocolate chip cookies as they are my favorite.

Peanut butter cookie S'mores my favorite S'more ever!

❖　❖　❖　❖

Banana Boats

This is a brilliant recipe I learned as a camp counselor. Not only is it a really tasty treat your kids will talk about for days but they are fun and easy to make.

Equipment

Foil
Knife

Ingredients

1 bag mini marshmallows
1 banana per person
1 package chocolate chips

Steps

Cut two slits on the banana along the inside curve of the banana about a half inch from each other, making sure to leave the peel intact. Hollow out about a quarter to half inch down of the banana where the slits were made. Fill in the banana with mini marshmallows and chocolate chips. Place the peel back over the ingredients and cover the banana with foil. I like to double wrap the foil on anything I toss directly on coals or fire so that it doesn't burn as easy. Cook for about 10 to 15 minutes or until the marshmallow and chocolate have melted. Let it sit for a few minutes after you remove from the fire to cool it down and so you don't burn yourself when you bite into that wonderful mix of marshmallow, chocolate and banana.

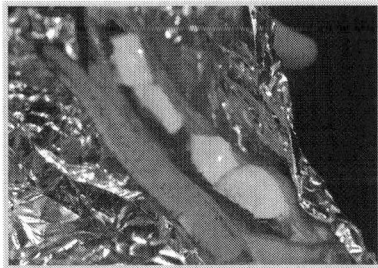

Banana Boat cooking in the coals of a fire.
The finished Banana Boat, use a spoon to eat.

Campfire Cake

Equipment

Dutch oven
Bowl

Ingredients

1 box cake mix

Steps

This is pretty simple. Grease your Dutch oven so the cake does not stick or if using a Dutch oven liner, grease it. In a bowl, mix a box of cake mix according to the directions. Pour into Dutch oven and bake at the specified temperature and time. You can use the chart in chapter 2 to determine the amount of coals for the specified temperature. When making a cake like this I also sometimes substitute the liquid in the mix recipe for Ginger Ale or a lime soda. Adding soda to the recipe increases the fluffiness of the cake and tastes great. Check that the cake is done by sticking a knife or toothpick into the dough. If it comes out clean then the cake is done. Let cool for about 10 or 15 minutes then turn Dutch oven over onto a plate. Let the cake cool completely and frost if desired.

The finished cake. I made this for a friend's birthday one summer while camping at Icicle Creek in Leavenworth.

❖   ❖   ❖   ❖

Fruit Pies

Equipment

Pie Iron or Dutch oven

Ingredients

1 can fruit
1 package puffed pastry dough
(thawed)

Steps

This is my favorite pie because the puffed pastry dough is so light and goes so well with the filling. The other great thing about puffed pastry is you can buy them pre-made from the frozen food section of your super market. Thaw the dough and cut it to the size of your choosing. Form the pies in to little pockets and place in a sprayed or greased Dutch oven being sure not to overcrowd. Bake at 400° using 29 coals with 19 on top and 10 on bottom for 15 minutes or until pie is golden brown.

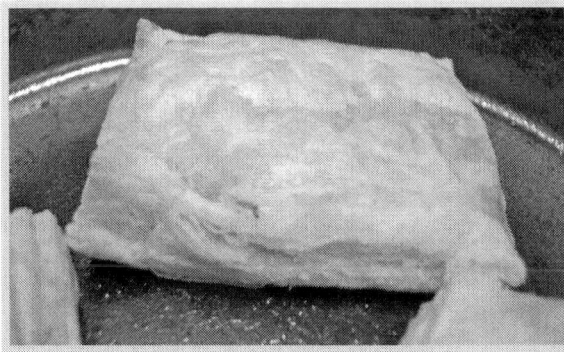

For these pies I cut one larger piece of puff pastry into three long strips, added filling to one side and folded over. I sealed in the seams with an egg wash. Use a fork to seal the sides for a nice touch.

❖　❖　❖　❖

Cinnamon Rolls

Equipment

Cast Iron Dutch
oven

Ingredients

1 package frozen
bread dough
(thawed)
2 tbsp. cinnamon
1 c. brown sugar

1 can vanilla frosting
1 tbsp. butter
½ c. walnuts
(optional)

Steps

Roll the dough out flat about ¼ inch think. Mix about 1 part brown sugar (you can also use a little white table sugar if you like) with 1 part cinnamon. Melt the butter and coat the rolled out dough liberally with it. Sprinkle the sugar cinnamon mixture on top of the dough, if you want to add nuts or mini chocolate chips you can do that now. Roll the dough up tightly but carefully and cut out 1 to 2 inch think pieces and place inside your greased Dutch oven. Rising time may vary according to room temperature, in general allow the dough to rise to about twice its original size. Place a lid on the Dutch oven and cook them at about 350° using 25 coals with 17 on top and 8 on bottom for about 20 minutes. Check for doneness and cook longer if needed to make sure they are golden brown and cooked through. These are easy to make in an RV oven as well.

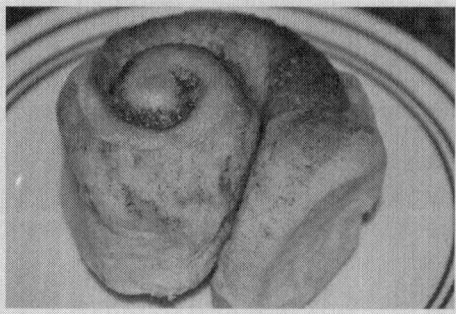

Let cool and add frosting. Be careful to make sure the roll is cooled enough before adding frosting or it will just melt off. But then again, that can be mighty tasty too.

❖   ❖   ❖   ❖

Sticky Bun on a Stick

Equipment

Marshmallow Roasting Stick

Ingredients

1 can biscuit dough
(pre-made or home-made)
2 tbsp. cinnamon
2 tbsp. sugar
1 tbsp. butter

Steps

Take your biscuit dough and wrap it around your cooking stick making sure it does not fall off. The thinner your wrap it the easier it will cook. Place over the fire or near some coals. Melt some butter in a pan and when the bun is browned roll it in the melted butter and then spread the cinnamon and sugar mixture over it. It's ready to eat as soon as it is cool enough.

❖　❖　❖　❖

Dutch oven Apple Pie

Equipment

Dutch oven

Ingredients

2 pre made pie crusts.
6 apples thinly sliced
1 c. sugar
2 tsp. cinnamon
½ tsp. nutmeg

Steps

Place the crust on the bottom of an aluminum pie pan or Dutch oven liner. The pan should easily fit in your oven. Mix together the filling of apples, sugar, cinnamon and nutmeg in a bowl. Add to the crust in the pan and take the remaining crust and place on top of filling. Beat the egg into an egg wash and baste the top dough with egg wash. Fold over the bottom dough over the top dough to seal the filling in. Cut 4 slits into the top dough for ventilation. Bake at 425° using 31 coals with 21 on top and 10 on bottom for 45 minutes to an hour until top crust is golden brown. Rotate the oven top to keep even browning on the crust.

❖　❖　❖　❖

Dutch Oven Berry Pie

Equipment

Dutch oven

Ingredients

2 ½ pre made pie crusts.
1 bag frozen berries
½ c. water
1 c. sugar
2 tsp. cinnamon (optional)

Steps

Place the crust on the bottom of an aluminum pie pan or Dutch oven liner. The pan liner should easily fit in your oven. If the Dutch oven liner is larger than the pie crust you will need to meld the pie crusts together to fit. Mix together the filling in a sauce pan over medium heat and add to the crust in the pan. Take remaining crust and place on top of filling. Beat the egg into an egg wash and baste the top dough with egg wash. Fold over the bottom dough over the top dough to seal the filling in. Cut slits into the top dough for ventilation. Bake at 425° using 31 coals with 21 on top and 10 on bottom for 45 minutes to an hour until top crust is golden brown. Rotate the oven top to keep even browning on the crust.

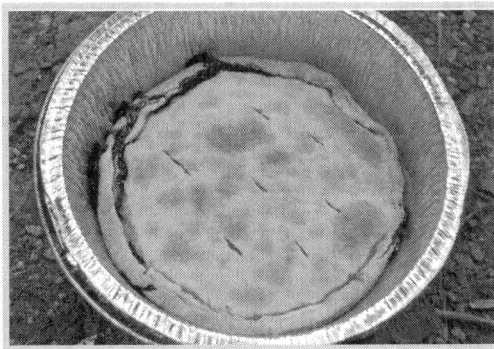

Berry pie where the crust was melded together to fit in a larger Dutch oven.

❖　❖　❖　❖

Coffee Can Ice Cream

Equipment

1 small coffee can
1 large coffee can

Ingredients

1 bag ice
Rock salt
1 cup half and half or cream
½ c. sugar
½ tsp. vanilla
1 maraschino cherry

Steps

Combine half and half, sugar and vanilla in smaller can. Seal tightly with lid. Place inside larger can and fill the large can sides all the way to the top with ice. Pour the salt over the ice and seal the big can tightly. You might consider duct taping it to keep it tightly shut. Roll the can around for about 10 minutes. Remove the smaller can and stir the ice cream. Replace lid and place back in the large can. Put more ice and salt around the smaller can, seal and roll around for another 5 or 10 minutes or until ice cream reaches the correct consistency. You can add other flavorings or toppings to give your ice cream your favorite flavor.

❖   ❖   ❖   ❖

Drunken Strawberry Shortcake

You will want to make sure the kids are in bed before you make this one. Please be responsible and don't allow those under 21 years of age to eat this dessert.

Equipment

Mixing bowl

Ingredients

2 c. strawberries, washed and sliced at least in half or quarters
1 can whipped cream
1 package of shortcake
1 cup bourbon or cognac

Steps

In a small mixing bowl place the strawberries and add a cup of bourbon and let soak in a cool location for at least an hour. Take a slice of shortcake and place it on a small plate or small shallow bowl. Spoon out the strawberries being sure not to get too much liquid or the cake will be soggy. Top with homemade or pre made whipped cream and top with the cherry. You can leave out the bourbon or cognac if serving to kids.

❖ ❖ ❖ ❖

Roasted Cream Filled Cake

Equipment

Marshmallow Roasting
Stick

Ingredients

1 box cream filled cake

Steps

Carefully place cake on roasting stick. Roast over fire till heated all the way through making sure not to burn the cake.

❖   ❖   ❖   ❖

Fire Roasted Apple

Equipment

Foil
Bowl

Ingredients

1 apple
1 tbsp. brown sugar
1 tsp. cinnamon
1 tbsp. chocolate syrup

Steps

Core the apple so that the middle is hollow. Mix the sugar and cinnamon in a bowl and place the mixture into the center of the apple. Wrap in foil and roast on coals for about 15 or 20 minutes. Carefully unwrap and drizzle with chocolate syrup. Let cool for a few minutes and serve warm.

❖   ❖   ❖   ❖

Grilled Peaches

Equipment

Grill Grate

Ingredients

2 large peaches
1 tsp. honey or chocolate syrup
1 tsp. canola oil or cooking spray

Steps

Preheat the grill to a medium heat. While the grill is heating cut the peaches in half and remove the pits. Lightly sprinkle the peach halves with canola oil or cooking spray. Soak some oil on a paper towel and wipe down the grill with towel or use cooking spray on the grill before placing the grill on the fire. Place the peaches on the grill with the cut side down for 2 to 3 minutes. Turn the peaches and cook another 2 minutes. Remove and drizzle with honey or chocolate syrup and serve.

❖   ❖   ❖   ❖

Camp Baked Peach

Equipment

Dutch Oven
Dutch Oven Aluminum
Liners or Cake Pan

Ingredients

½ stick butter
4 cups peaches,
peeled and sliced (or canned)
1 c. sugar
1 c. flour
1 c. milk
1 tbsp. honey

Steps

Melt the butter in the liner or cake pan. Add the peaches and sugar and mix in the flour and then the milk. Place the pan in the Dutch oven, cover and bake in the coals at around 350° using 25 coals with 17 on top and 8 on bottom for about 35 minutes. Alternatively you can use the Dutch oven without the liner or cake pan but cleanup is much easier with a liner.

❖   ❖   ❖   ❖

Fruit Crisp

Equipment

Dutch Oven

Ingredients

1 or 2 cans of fruit pie filling
¾ c. of butter
¾ c. of brown sugar
1 ¼ c. of flour
¾ c. of oats
1 tbsp. cinnamon

Steps

Fill bottom of Dutch oven with the fruit pie filling. Combine brown sugar, flour, oats and cinnamon. Cut butter into the dry ingredients and spread over the top of the fruit. Cover oven and bake at 350° using 25 coals with 17 on top and 8 on the bottom for about 45 minutes or until fruit is soft.

❖   ❖   ❖   ❖

Fruit Cobbler

Equipment

Dutch Oven
Liner

Ingredients

2 cans sliced fruit
(use fruit with syrup base)
1 c. biscuit mix

Steps

Spray some not stick spray into the bottom of a Dutch oven or use a Dutch oven liner and spray the liner. Drain ¼ cup of the syrup from the fruit cans but save the syrup and set aside. Mix the ¼ cup of syrup with biscuit mix until it forms a batter type consistency. Pour batter back over fruit. Cover oven and bake at 350° using 25 coals with 17 on top and 8 on the bottom for about 45 minutes or until the batter is formed into dumplings.

❖   ❖   ❖   ❖

Dutch Oven Stickies

Equipment

Dutch Oven

Ingredients

2 cans buttermilk biscuits
½ c. sugar
2 tbsp. cinnamon
2 tbsp. butter
1 c. walnuts (optional)
1 can frosting or glaze (optional)

Steps

Mix the cinnamon and sugar together in a bowl. Cut the biscuits into quarters and dip in sugar cinnamon mixture and then place in a greased Dutch oven leaving an open space in the middle. Melt the butter and drizzle over the biscuits top with nuts if desired. Cover with lid and cook for about 45 minutes at 400° using 29 coals with 19 on top and 10 on bottom. Let cool for about 10 minutes and drizzle with frosting or glaze if desired.

❖   ❖   ❖   ❖

Fried Apple Pie

Equipment

Rolling Pin
Cast Iron Fry Pan

Ingredients

1 can biscuits
1 can apple pie filling
1 tbsp. white sugar
1 tbsp. cinnamon
1 or 2 tbsp. canola oil

Steps

Mix cinnamon and sugar together in a container and set mixture aside. Roll a biscuit out flat and place pie filling in the middle. Cover the biscuit and filling by folding over and pressing down the edges, use a fork to seal the edges and make sure filling does not leak out the edges. Heat pan with oil and when the oil is hot place the pie into the pan. Cook until browned, turn and brown the other side. Remove and immediately sprinkle with cinnamon and sugar mixture. Let cool for a few minutes and serve. Pie filling will be very hot.

I used two biscuits for this pie. One biscuit works better
and will be less doughy.

❖　❖　❖　❖

Salted Caramel Chocolate Pecan Pie

Equipment

Pie Pan
Cast Iron Dutch Oven

Ingredients

Chocolate Filling
1 1/2 cup sugar
3/4 cups butter (melted)
1/3 cup all-purpose flour
1/2 cup 100% unsweetened cocoa
1 or 2 shakes of ghost salt
1 tablespoon light corn syrup
1 teaspoon vanilla extract
3 large eggs
1 cup toasted chopped pecans
one 9-inch crust

Salted Caramel Topping
3/4 cups sugar
1 tablespoon fresh lemon juice
1/4 cup water
1/3 cup heavy cream
4 tablespoons butter
1/4 teaspoon table salt
2 cups toasted pecan halves
1/2 teaspoon sea salt

I made this pie in my RV. This can also be done in a Dutch oven.

Steps

Chocolate Filling

Preheat oven to 350° F or start your fire. Stir together sugar, butter, flour, cocoa, corn syrup, and vanilla extract in a large bowl. Add eggs and whip until everything has blended. Add chopped pecans, mix, and pour into pie shell. Bake at 350° for 35 - 40 minutes. If using a Dutch oven bake at 350° using 25 coals with 17 on top and 8 on bottom for 35 - 40 minutes. The filling will seem uncooked, this is normal, it will harden as it cools. Cool on a wire rack.

Salted Caramel Topping

Bring the sugar, lemon juice and water to boil in a saucepan over a camp stove. Be sure not to stir the mixture, just swirl the pot from time to time. Watch for the sugar to change color to a nice brown and continue for 8 minutes. Remove from heat and add butter. When butter has melted slowly add cream. Continuously stir the mixture until boiling stops and all ingredients are mixed. Stir in table salt. Arrange pecan halves on top of the chocolate filling. Top the pecans with the caramel mixture. Let the pie cool for 15-30 minutes before sprinkling the sea salt on top. The caramel mixture will thicken and keep the pecans in place.

❖   ❖   ❖   ❖

Appendix

Cleaning & Filleting, Fish & Seafood

Preparing seafood can be a messy job. It is not really all that difficult however, and if you want the best tasting freshest seafood you should definitely try to catch it yourself or at least purchase it from a good fish monger. Fish and seafood is better freshly cleaned and prepared, so knowing how to properly prepare fish will help your meals be outstanding.

No matter what sort of preparations you are making, start with a large plastic cutting board and a sharp, high quality fillet knife about 8 inches long. Plastic cutting boards are preferable for use in preparing fish because they will not absorb any foulness from the fish. Using newspaper to line the table underneath your cutting board is a good idea to soak up any mess.

How to Clean and Gut Fish

On the underbelly of the fish, centered, but toward the tail, is a small spot, possibly indented and/or colored slightly differently than the belly. This is the anus of the fish, and it is where you begin to remove innards. Start by placing the knife tip about an inch deep into the anus (depending on the size of the fish). Slice a straight line upward towards the head until you reach the gills. The fish should open up to reveal the organs; if it does not you haven't cut deeply enough. Cut the gills out and pull the organs out of the fish, leaving the spine and ribs exposed. Then dig out the blood vessels alongside the spine.

To scale the fish take a butter knife and grab the fish with one hand, with the other hand holding the knife rub the skin of the fish from tail to head. Be sure to get all parts of the fish including the spine and tail. At this point you can cut off the head and tail but some people prefer to leave it attached. Keeping the head on will not hurt anything but for some the gross factor is too much to handle.

How to Fillet Fish

Start by cleaning and gutting your fish before proceeding with the next step. You can read about how to do this in the above section.

With the fish in front of you with the belly facing you, cut just behind the gill bone, cutting at a slight angle towards the head until you reach the backbone. Be sure you do not cut through the backbone. Now make sure the thin part of the meat of the belly is cut free. While holding the belly part above the knife blade, turn the knife edge toward the tail so that it is parallel to the backbone. Now cut towards the tail while holding up the belly using the bone as your guide towards the tail. Once you reach the dorsal fin, be sure to leave the fin on the backbone. At this point you will be cutting through some rib bones but muscle it through to the tail and cut through to the tail at the very end making sure to keep as much meat on the fillet as possible. Now flip the fish over and cut behind the other gill to the backbone again. Again lift the belly meat up and turn the knife edge toward the tail. Angle the knife enough that you retain the most meat possible from the carcass. Again cut through to the tail leaving the anal fin attached to the carcass. If you are inclined you can save the carcass as it makes great crab bait!

To remove the remaining rib bones from the fillets place a fillet with the meat side up on the cutting board. Have the thick part of the meat closest to you so that the belly is away from you. Remove the first couple of ribs closest to where the head end was. Then angle the knife under the ribs starting at the backbone side. Be sure to angle the knife into the ribs so you do not remove too much meat. Then follow the ribs toward the belly cutting as you go. Trim any visible ribs remaining. Now cut any fins remaining on the filet, remove ribs from second fillet, rinse and you are done.

How to Clean a Cooked Crab

Once crab is cooked, it must be cleaned. To clean the crab, flip it over on its stomach and place your thumb under the flap on the underside of the crab. This is called the apron. Males have a narrow apron and females have a wider one. In most areas females are supposed to be thrown back if caught, so you will most likely have a male crab.

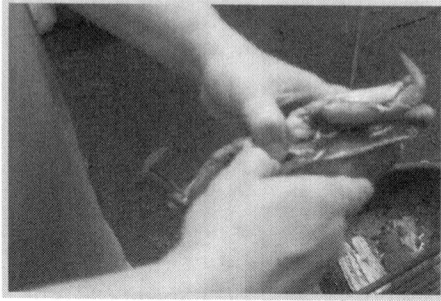

Pull off the apron and place your thumb into the hole left from removing it. Pull off the top shell (carapace) from the crab. This detaches much of the undesirables from the crab meat.

Next you must remove any intestines left inside, and remove the gills from the body. These are the spongy streaks on either side and are not good to eat. You can also wash away the crab butter, the yellow mushy stuff running down the center of the crab, but some consider this a delicacy so you can set it aside if you like. Finally, remove the mouth parts from the body and rinse the body well with water.

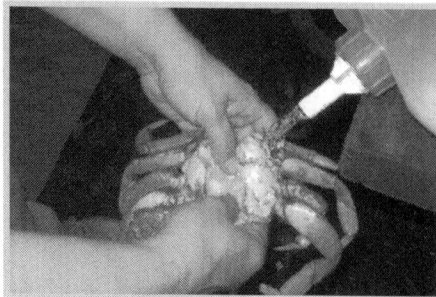

The legs and claws can be twisted off and served separately, or the crab can be served whole and cracked open. Serve with melted butter.

How to Clean Razor Clams

Soak the clams in cold fresh water for about 30 minutes before cleaning. This often will cause the clams to release any sand still left in their bodies. With a sharp knife, carefully cut open the clam. Slice the clam body free of the shell and then trim off anything that looks black. Rinse and cook as desired.

How to Clean Shrimp

Shrimp and crab are the foods that really need to be fresh-caught to be at its most delectable. If you can get a mess of fresh-caught shrimp, you will need to clean and devein it, but even shrimp that you buy from the store often needs cleaning.

First you will need to separate the head from the shrimp. You can simply pull it off (it will detach fairly easily), or if you feel squeamish about that method, cut it off, and discard it. Next, pull the legs off and peel the shrimp's shell away from the body. Some folks like to leave a little shell on the end of the tail; the choice is yours. Next, devein the shrimp by cutting a slit about a quarter inch deep along the back of the shrimp with a small, sharp knife. You should see the black vein and can then take the knife and pry it out. If you do not see a vein, don't worry; they do not always have one. Finally, rinse the shrimp and it should be ready for cooking.

How to Clean Squid

To clean squid, I recommend that you wear an apron and cover your work surface with newspaper since this can be a messy job.

The first step is to remove the head from the body. Grasp the squid with one hand on either side of the line where the head joins the body, and firmly but gently twist and pull the head off with your hands. The innards should come sliding out, attached to the head, as you pull. If the ink sac breaks, the ink can simply be rinsed away; if not, you can reserve the ink for later use by cutting the small, silvery sac free.

The edible tentacles of the squid are attached to the head just below the eyes, rather than to the body; cut them off next, as close to the eye as possible.

At the base of the tentacles is a boney piece of cartilage which looks somewhat like a mushroom. This is the beak, and you should remove and discard it as well.

At the top of the body there is a tube, within which is a thin piece of cartilage. Grasp the cartilage, pull it out of the tube, and discard.

Cut or peel away the side fins. Depending on the type of squid you are cooking, you may need to remove the skin as well. Some species of squid have edible skin; if you know that yours is one of these then you may choose to skip this step.

Finally, check to make sure no bits of innards remain inside the body, and rinse the squid.

Shucking Oysters and Clams

When attempting to shuck shell fish I recommend a good pair of gloves to protect your hands. A towel will work as well but you will be better protected with a good pair of gloves. Leather will work but I prefer cut resistant gloves. You will also need a good shucking knife. You may want to work over a bowl or sink as shucking can get messy. To shuck, hold the hinge of the shell in front of you and place the knife in the hinge of the shell and work the shell open. Once the hinge releases the rest of the shell will come apart fairly easily. You can remove the meat for your recipe or roast the oyster in the shell on a barbeque. If you like oysters raw you can add a little hot sauce and lemon juice and serve right from the half shell.

Measurement Equivalents

3 Teaspoons = 1 Tablespoon

4 Tablespoon = ¼ Cup

5 1/3 Tablespoons = 1/3 Cup

8 Tablespoons = ½ Cup

12 Tablespoons = ¾ Cup

16 Tablespoons = 1 Cup

1 Fluid Ounce = 2 Tablespoons

8 Fluid Ounces = 1 Cup = ½ Pint

16 Fluid Ounces = 2 Cups = 1 Pint

32 Fluid Ounces = 1 Quart = 2 Pints

128 Fluid Ounces = 1 Gallon = 4 Quarts

Food Safety

Food safety outdoors is much the same as it would be in any kitchen, that being said, there are some situations around a campsite that are unique to food safety. The author and publisher of this book take no responsibility for food safety and mention it as a service to the reader.

First there are a few basic rules to food safety.

1. Keep it clean. Keep hands and working surfaces clean before and after preparation. When camping, it's a good idea to have

a clean water pale or pot for washing. I also keep a good supply of wet wipes for my hands when I cannot readily wash them. Latex gloves are also a great way to keep clean when working with chicken or other meats.

2.   Separate, and do not cross contaminate. Any time raw meat, poultry, seafood and eggs touch a surface that area should be cleaned.

3.   Cook the food to the correct temperature to destroy harmful bacteria.

4.   Chill the food. Keep food chilled before cooking and chill leftovers immediately once they are cooled.

Aside from these basics you should also learn the safest way to thaw food, use plenty of soap and water when cleaning and throw out any food you think may be tainted or smells funny. This is especially true if you are storing your food in coolers where the ice may have melted and the water from the melted ice contaminates other foods in the cooler. Coolers should always be placed in the shade to keep the ice in tact longer.

One way to keep food from becoming contaminated it to store it in a zip lock bag. This helps reduce the amount of contamination from melted ice. Also, drain any water from the cooler as soon as you replace it to reduce the amount of water in the cooler. It is important to clean your cooler at the end of your trip to reduce any possible bacteria left behind.

Meat must always be handled with care and it's a good idea to have some way to disinfect your preparation surfaces after you are done working. Also, be sure to wash your food before you prepare it. This will help reduce the amount of bacteria before cooking. Please note, that meats do not need washing but vegetables should always be washed. Washing meats may spread contamination when the water for the rinse splatters. If you choose to wash, do so carefully.

Seafood and poultry are not only best when they are fresh, they are safest when they are fresh. Shellfish can be especially dangerous if not harvested from safe beaches that have been approved by authorities. Never harvest seafood without a license and the knowledge that red tide or other toxins do not exist on the beach. If buying seafood, buy it alive, flash frozen at the time it was caught or caught the day you plan to cook it. Many stores sell live seafood; so keep the seafood alive as long as possible.

Keep eggs in a cooler and never let any item sit out for too long. Never put hot food in a cooler, always let it cool first and place it in the cooler as soon as possible.

When handling foods while camping, I often use disposable latex gloves to keep my hands from touching the food since camping can be a dirty activity with few places to wash available. The great thing about using surgeon's gloves is when you are handling dangerous raw foods such as chicken it's easier to keep your hands from becoming contaminated. Be sure to use powder free gloves for cooking. Keeping soap and water or soapy wipes on hand are also a must.

One last thing to remember: **When in doubt, throw it out!**

Food Storage – How long should I keep that?

General guidelines for how long to keep food may not apply to you as a camper because of the fact your cooler may not be at 40° F as a refrigerator should be.

The following are for raw food held in a refrigerator at 40° F.
Bacon: 7 days
Sausage: 1 or 2 days

Smoked Sausage: 7 days

Ham (cooked): 7 days

Hot Dogs: 1 week opened, 2 weeks unopened

Lunch Meats: 2 week opened, 3 weeks unopened

Raw Beef: 3 to 5 days

Raw Lamb: 3 to 5 days

Raw Pork: 3 to 5 days

Ground Beef: 2 days

Poultry: 2 days

Fish: 1 to 2 days

The following are storage times for leftovers.

Chicken: 3 to 4 days

Meat: 3 to 4 days

Soups: 4 days

Again if it smells bad it probably is bad and should be thrown out.

Cutting up a Chicken

There are several ways to cut up a whole chicken into parts. This is my method. Use a heavy butcher knife for cutting chicken and for safety, make sure your knife is sharp. Most cutting accidents happen with dull knives.

- On a cutting board with the chicken back side down, cut through the center of the breast and down on one side of the backbone.

- Next cut through the other side of the back bone to remove it from the chicken. (This bone is great for stock if you want to save it)

- Cut through skin and meat between the thigh and the breast. Pull the leg back and cut through the joint of the thigh and the breast.

- Now cut between the thigh and the leg at the joint to separate.

- Cut off the wing from the breast.

- Cut the breast in half. (Or you can leave the breast whole)

Removing Membrane from Spare Ribs

There is a little secret that good barbeque people know about making great ribs. This is a really quick trick that will help make your ribs all the more tender.

Take your ribs at biggest end and either use a knife or your finger and loosen underneath the membrane trying not to rip it. Gently pull the membrane up trying to keep it in tack as you pull. Once you have a good grip on the membrane continue pulling it back until you have pulled it off the entire rack. Now you are ready to add your rub and cook the ribs.

Why let my meat rest?

Meat continues to cook when you remove it from the heat so by removing your meat a little early from its desired doneness you give it a chance to complete the cooking process. Most experts say to remove a roast about 5° to 10° degrees before it is done. This also lets the moisture in the meat settle back down into the tissue helping to retain the juices. Always let your meat stand.

Choosing a good camp stove

For the type of cooking in this book you will want to choose a good stove with heat control levers and a stable base. Here are some different choices for the different type of camping you may encounter.

Back Packing: Back packing stoves are generally small and used mostly for boiling water for hot beverages or water for cooking dehydrated foods. These can be as small as a canister or can have a chamber for the fuel. Some even have wood burning capabilities.

Car Camping: This is usually the weekender who spends about 2 evenings on average out in the woods, camps in a tent and brings many comforts such as a cooler and table and chairs. The typical stove that works well for this type of camper is the two burner propane stove. A one burner stove also works well but two burners are often preferred so you can make coffee while making breakfast at the same time.

Recreational Vehicle: The last type of typical stove out there for camping is for those who are on longer trips last more than 2 or 3 days. These are often RVrs who stay in camp sites for extended periods. The RV enthusiast brings many comforts of home with them on their trip including BBQ's and multi burner propane stoves. RVs often come with a built in stove and oven as well.

There are many more types of stoves out there to choose from. The best thing to do is to consider the type of camping you intend to spend the most time at and go with that. The great thing about BBQs is that they can also be used as a stove for some items. And the multi burner stove is handy to setup for large crowds and is comfortable to use when it is a free standing unit. Either of these are great for car camping or RVing.